DIARY

OF THE CAJUN

MOUNTAIN MAN

WRITTEN BY:
JAMES W HALE
(THE CAJUN MOUNTAIN MAN)
1981 - 1982

PHOTOGRAPHS BY:
JAMES W HALE

BOOK DESIGNED &
PUBLISHED BY:
LISA HALE GALLAGHER
2019

EMAIL CONTACT
DIARYOFTHECAJUNMOUNTAINMAN@OUTL
OOK.COM

PRINTED IN THE UNITED STATES OF
AMERICA
FIRST PUBLISHED 2019 AMAZON / KINDLE
ISBN 9781692597764

My name is Lisa Gallagher. This is my father's diary that I found after he passed away in 2008. It was also kind of my way of coping with his loss. May God give him eternal life in heaven. And this book give him eternal life in everyone's hearts. This book can answer so many questions that I am asked all the time. About; how can one man build such a beautiful cabin with no power tools? How did he survive against all of those predators up there? How did he come to find this beautiful place? And other questions about. When he was tossed around for 17 hours in the Gulf of Mexico, during a fierce Gulf storm. With waves so high. He barely had time to take a breath  between the waves crashing over his head. Punching sharks away from him with his bare hands. And being run over by a large boat. Kicking the hull and barely missing the propeller. And so many people loved his photography, which sold for hundreds of dollars. He knew the swamps of Louisiana like the back of his hand. He went places in the swamps that most if the locals feared to go. And would spend the night on his boat in the swamp. Just to wake up and get the perfect photo. Just to share this beauty with others. And he always wanted to make a book of the outhouses of the North Fork. But God took him before he could finish it. So I decided to incorporate all of this and more into this book. The pictures were the hardest part because almost all of these photos were taken before digital cameras and computers existed. And not many people develop this size negative anymore. They are not the regular size negatives that we see with today's 35mm cameras. I'm not a photographer. I did my best. He could have defiantly done better. A TV producer contacted him once. Wanting to do a story about his life. He declined. He said that there was no way they could sum it all up in 30 minutes. So, I dedicate this to him. The man that I believed to be invincible, my Daddy, James Hale "The Cajun Mountain Man"   I hope you like it,

Lisa Hale Gallagher

4

A bearded Montana man, standing in snow, is a far cry from a coat-and-tie insurance executive in hot and humid Lafayette.

A Lafayette businessman finds his own Walden Pond amidst the
mountains and snow of Montana and manages to find
The Essentials of Life….and himself.

Gold and silver may have earned Montana its nickname "The Treasure
State," but Lafayette Louisiana insurance agent finds much more of value
there since forsaking the rat race in 1981 to build a Rocky Mountain retreat.

Two acres around rugged, yet peaceful Glacier National Park are Jim Hale's
personal Shangri-La

Hand Built (no power tools) by Hale over 10 months' time, a pine cabin in
northwestern Montana provides the retreat he wants, needs and appreciates.

"I think we all have the drive to get away from it all" The 44 year old
business man said, "I just did something about it."

"Something" was taking a year's leave from work, heading north with little
more than ambition and building the cabin we now call "The Cajun
Hideaway."

Clean shaven and suited, Jim Hale in Lafayette looks remarkably different
from the bearded, cap-on-head, gun in hand hunter photographed in late 1981

Hale pursued his adventure like Henry David Thoreau. Who found it was
time to "front the essentials of life" with a cabin on Walden Pond.

An insurance agent for 20-plus years, native to Lafayette and New Iberia
Louisiana area and divorced father of two, he had been in the mountains
for only short stays before.

"We'd go every year, into the woods on a hunt or something," he said. "It
was wonderful – so much more diversification in animals, climate, scenery,
lifestyle and challenges than the flatlands….But it was never long enough."

Forty years old at the time, Hale realized "if you want to make your dreams
come true, you sometimes have to make a supreme effort."

"I think we all have the drive to get away from it all.
I just did something about it." There were probably three years of serious
thought behind that effort before it came to fruition, he figured;
"Then it was like a bomb ready to go off"
"Nothing in particular happened," he said. "Mentally, I was just
ready….though I felt the world would fall apart around me when I left."

6

He took provisions and 17-year old son Kevin out of Lafayette May 1st 1981, at first for a trip into the wilderness of British Columbia, Canada.

Not being Canadian meant Hale couldn't get a job, much less buy land to build a permanent structure. A tour of Canada and 20 miles southward later, he and Kevin crossed back into the United States and northwestern Montana.

"We just kind of followed our noses into the area," Hale explained. "It's the last stronghold of the grizzly bear, "40 miles from the nearest town and almost a mile to the nearest neighbor.

He found two acres of land available for purchase – a feat in itself, considering the federal government owns upwards of 90 percent of the land and vacant private property is limited.

The Cajun businessman paid $4,000 an acre, which he agrees was high at the time, even for prime woodland. Other plots were going for $1,000 an acre.

"But it's worth more than $4,000 an acre to me" he said. "Even worth more than the additional $2,000 you might tack on" as an estimate of the cabin investment alone, he told the interviewer Donna Fontenot.

Two other Louisiana friends sent money to Montana, site unseen.

Said one, Kaplan insurance associate Freddie Hebert, after a few cabin visits: "It's everything I thought it would be, and every penny – and more – worth my investment....they really did a great job."

Hale and his son started building July 1, 1981, without the aid of power tools and in an area devoid of electrical services and telephones.

Permanent structures couldn't be built in national forests. Tree-cutting permits had to be obtained; and even then big trees couldn't indiscriminately be chopped down. Governmental agencies control land use. "There's a lot involved," Hale commented. "Even away from civilization, you have rules and regulations to abide by...."We're more socialized than we think."

"Building a log cabin is nothing like building a house, either," he adds.

Even with background as a contractor's son, Hale had much to learn.

Logs – some of them weighing 800 pounds each – had to be hauled in and peeled with a draw knife. An interim "tepee" had to be built to protect food that bears once tried eating out of Hale's pickup truck. An angered bull elk attacked once.

Hale spent six months of his initial 10-month stay living out of a tent and most of it alone.

He and Kevin had returned to Louisiana briefly in August when Hale's father died; and Kevin was unable to go back because of a new school term. Hale returned to a pine framework that was only 4 logs high. He built the rest alone – "every day for those 10 months" – eventually completing a 17 by 21 foot base and a loft half that size for a two story cabin.

Lights and stove are powered by butane.

"I hadn't intended to build such an elaborate cabin," Hale said. "I initially just wanted it away from the bears and the cold, perhaps something temporary that I could tear down or burn later."

"I built what I did out of necessity," he added. "I'd put so much into it by then, meeting all the regulations and stuff, it wasn't worth just a 'quickie'."

Quick is not an adjective Hale is likely to use in describing any facet of his Montana life.

There is plenty of time to learn ice skating, snow skiing and snowmobiling, days between Tuesday and Friday mail deliveries in the nearest town, sometimes a week before he sees someone to talk to, and up to a month at times between visits into town.

Hale keeps a daily journal, takes pictures, writes poetry and "plays a little" in Montana besides.

"You don't get bored," he said. "But you get out there and you have to play a little."

Recreation might mean, as it did one day, photographing a real-live chicken on mini-snow skis for subsequent reproduction onto t-shirts for friends. ("Just fun," said the insurance salesman who once "captured" a frog on a motorcycle for the 1980 Rayne Frog Festival poster.)

"The biggest thing I had a problem with was not the hard work or the bitter cold," Hale reflected. It was warm when we went up and we had provisions we needed, plus an understanding of hypothermia and survival techniques.

"The worst thing, by far; is the loneliness," he added.

When you're alone, you worry if there'll be anyone around in case you get hurt. It makes you think a lot more, and you become cautious….You become half wild." Hale commented. "It surprised me I didn't confine my words, actions or dress to be socially acceptable like in the big city."

It makes returning to the Lafayette business world tough at times, he admitted. "Much tougher than leaving – and almost like reverse culture shock."

"But money's got to be made…..Work time goes by fast. I like my work, and can now do it knowing I've something to work for."

DIARY
OF THE CAJUN
MOUNTAIN MAN

{JAMES W. HALE}

Tuesday 6/16/81

Today at 11:30 a.m. I leave on a trip to British Columbia, Canada, with intentions of returning to Lafayette, La. a year from now. I am accompanied by my son Kevin who will spend the summer with me. I leave my Mom and Dad, my girlfriend of 3 years, my friends, my business associates and a relatively comfortable life to live in the most remote mountain wilderness that I can find in British Columbia. I have thought about doing this for several years and decided a few months ago that now is the time to do it. I have spent 3 solid non-stop months preparing for this year, and now finally we are on our way. There seems to be a very strong drive inside of me to step out of society for a time and live with nature. It is as though I am on the threshold of some of life's answers (at least for me) and perhaps they can be found in nature. I really don't know what waits for me - I only know there is a strong drive behind it all. As we leave Lafayette it is very coincidental that we meet on I-10 my immediate boss & good friend, Willie East. He was the only person I really needed to see and could not find. I briefed him on what needed to be done in my insurance business, bid him good-bye, and was on my way. The weather was clear, sultry and hot. The truck was running a little hot but still OK. We got to my brother, David's house in Dallas, Texas about 9:30 p.m.

Wednesday 6/17/81

We leave Dallas about 8:30 a.m. The weather cool until 11 a.m. or so then it got hot and dry. We stopped about 3:30 p.m. to eat a bite. The wind was

blowing so hard, it blew Kevin's sandwich off the roadside table. We had to hold our canned drinks so they wouldn't blow off too. It was so hot and dry that the bread was like toast after 5 minutes. We took the thermostat out of the engine, hoping it would help the truck run cooler. Didn't help much though. In the panhandle of Texas we came by a large sprinkler on wheels that was used to water a large corn field. We took off our shirts and shoes and took an outdoor shower right in the middle of the corn field.

People on the road would blow their horns and wave as they went by. The water was cold and refreshing. We drove through the pass north of Raton, NM. And into Colorado where we found a spot off the road to pitch the tent. The night was cool and the moon was full. The sky was so clear and the moon

so bright that it cast shadows like the early morning sun. The night was pretty, the temperature about 55 or 60°. We slept out under the stars instead of in the tent.

Royal Gorge Bridge
Can you see the giant face below the bridge?

Jim's Truck on the bridge

Thursday 6/18/81

Woke up about 9 a.m. and drove to Canon City, Co. Visited Royal Gorge & the world's highest suspension bridge. We rode the tram to the bottom of the Gorge & the cable car across the top. We then went to the town of Buckskin Joe where several movies were filmed. We spent several hours here. This is a replica of an actual old west boom town. We watched one of the top 5 magicians in the world, saw 3 well staged gunfights, and in general enjoyed the whole town. Drove to Aspen Co. that night and slept in White River National Forest campground "difficult." Again we slept out under the stars.

Friday 6/19/81

Spent the morning in Aspen. This is a very clean, colorful and modern looking town. Although the ski lifts were closed, the town seemed packed with people. The right front tire on the truck was getting a strange wear pattern on the outside treads. We tightened the bearings a little and had the tier flipped over & remounted. Drove to Dinosaur National Monument that night. Saw three deer & ran into two birds. Slept in a campground in Dinosaur National Monument near Jensen, Utah. P.S. – at campground "difficult." This morning we took a bath in a backwoods stream. The water was so cold it would not lather the soap. It seemed colder than ice.

Saturday 6/20/81

Woke up to the singing of birds, chipmunks running around our sleeping bags, a warm clear sunny sky - a perfect day. Drove around Dinosaur National Park - a lot of nothing. However, the excavation site was interesting. Went to Flaming Gorge National Recreation Area in Wyoming. The Flaming Gorge dam was interesting. Drove on to the Grand Tetons & slept in the Jenny Lake Campground in the Grand Teton National Park. It was sprinkling rain so we slept in the tent.

Sunday 6/21/81

Up at 9AM with the weather cool. Drove around the park, took some pictures of the Tetons. Drove to Grant Village and secured a campsite at the campground there. Went to see Old Faithful, Gibbon Falls and all the geyser basins up to Norris. (In Yellowstone National Park) We drove back to Grant Village at night. As we were talking we somehow missed our turn & ended up at the south entrance of Yellowstone. It was 12 midnight & we were low on gas. We made it back to the campsite though & went to bed about 1 a.m. The ranger said a bear had been in the camp the night before & for all campers to be alert. He didn't come back - we were hoping he would.

Monday 6/22/8

1woke up about 9 a.m. Adjusted toe-in on truck, placed boat battery in truck to charge it, filled up with gas & headed up the east road to see Upper & Lower Falls, Tower Falls, & Mammoth Hot Springs.

Yesterday & today we saw several elk, moose, ducks, buffalo and coyotes. Got several good shots of them with the camera. Drove on to Helena, Montana. We couldn't find a good place to sleep ended up near a "babbling" brook in someone's wheat ranch at 1p.m. Slept like a log.

Tuesday 6/23/81
We were awakened about 8:30AM by someone hollering "hey" at us. I was the ranch owner & he wanted to know what we were doing there. He had his hands on a pistol in his back pocket. He was relieved when we told him we hadn't been able to find a place to camp & had just stopped to sleep. He just didn't know what we were up to & was leery. He seemed a nice guy & talked to us quite a while about the fires in Napa Valley, the floods around Montana, etc.

We drove on to the Canadian border near Sweet Grass. Had the left front tire flipped over & remounted, changed the oil & headed on across the border. Spent about 1 hour in customs but no real problems. Slept in a Travel Lodge in Calgary, Alberta, Ca

Wednesday 6/24/81

Tried to get in touch with the pilot who was to take us flying over British Columbia. Spent the time seeing the sights in Calgary, washing our clothes & shopping. Still was unable to contact our pilot. Slept at the La Concha Motel.

Thursday 6/25/81

Finally got in touch with the pilot (Rick Martsolf) about 10 a.m. He had been working on one of his airplanes until after midnight each night. He won't be able to take us over British Columbia until Tuesday. We want to see Banff & Lake Louise area so we decide to spend the next four days there & then return to Calgary. The plane can save us a lot of time so we will wait until Tuesday. We arrive in Banff by mid-afternoon, secure a campsite right outside of town and spend the rest of the day shopping & seeing the sights around Banff. We return to the camp about 9 p.m. The sun sets here at about 10 p.m. and it doesn't get really dark until around 11 p.m. We build a fire and have hot dogs for supper. There are a few mosquitoes here so we will have to sleep in the tent.

Friday 6/26/81
We strike camp about 9 a.m. and go to the ski lift at Mt. Norquay just outside of Banff. Took some pictures of bighorn sheep on the slopes there.

We then drove to Lake Louise & secured a campsite. We would prefer to camp other than in a campground, but government regulation here strictly forbids camping other than in a campground in any National Park. Took some pictures of several ground squirrels. They were so unafraid of man that they would crawl in the cookie box and get themselves a cookie, or they would take one out of your hand.

We went to the lake (Lake Louise) and it is the prettiest area (mountain area) that I have ever seen. A clear blue-green lake surrounded by steep cliff - shrouded snowcapped mountains. We walked around the lake and up to a tea house that was built at the end of a small glacier. The walk was 7 miles round trip. We played in the snow at the end of the glacier (about 10' to 15' thick) for a while & then had some hot chocolate & soup at the tea house. Went back to the campsite, built a fire & had hot dogs & ham sandwiches

Saturday 6/27/81

It sprinkled rain during the night. We awoke to a cloudy threatening sky. Went back to Lake Louise to take a picture of the mountains covered with clouds. Ate at a rip-off cafeteria in Lake Louise. Drove to Athabasca Glacier.

Slid down the glacier a few time & threw a few snowballs at each other. Got all wet. On the way to secure a campsite we drove into a snowstorm. (In June! - can't believe it). It was wet snow & melted as soon as

it fell. The campsite was on a hill near a rushing stream. We walked (climbed) halfway up the mountain when we noticed another snowstorm approaching. We hurried to get down & put up the tent. Before the tent was up though it began to snow heavily. The snow was sort of white fluffy little balls like broken up Styrofoam. It covered the ground in about 5 minutes – then it stopped. Kevin tried for an hour & a half to light a fire, before he finally got it going. The only wood we had was some freshly cut "green" pine that would not light. It had turned cold now & was snowing a wet snow. We cooked a couple of pieces of ham & went to bed.

Sunday 6/28/81

Woke up to a sun shining day. The sky was partly cloudy. Went for a snow cat ride on Athabasca Glacier. Found a steep slope & slid down a few times - got all wet again. Drove on to Jasper, Alberta, Ca. saw a couple of good waterfalls on the way. Also, got some pictures of a couple of bull elk. Set up camp in a campsite just outside of Jasper. Kevin has been having fun with a puppet monkey he bought in Banff. People stop & look trying to figure out what it is - it looks real, but not just like a monkey. Kevin calls it a yampi. The lady at the campsite ticket office told us that there were bears in the campground & we should keep our pet confined. We told her he liked bears & was our protection. Finally she asked us if it was a dog or what. We didn't say - just said it was friendly. It took her several minutes before she realized that it wasn't real. She had a good laugh. We did too. Went to Whistlers Mountain & to town for groceries. Not much here to interest us. Went to camp early to build a fire & eat.

Monday 6/29/81

Today we must alter our plans. Last night we called the pilot in Calgary & his airplane is still down. He had to order a part for it & it may be a week or more before it comes in. We decide to head down to Kimberly, B.C. where we plan to build our log cabin. Perhaps we can find someone else there who can take us up. On the way to Lake Louise we stop to get some pictures of a huge & beautiful bull elk. At first he was lying down just chewing his cud. But there were other people around taking pictures also & he got up as we got closer. I followed him into the woods and snuck up behind him.

When he turned around, I laid down on the ground to get an upward shot on him. He must have thought I was crouching down to spring on him, and he charged. I quickly scampered behind a thick cluster of aspens nearby. At least here he couldn't get to me with his big antlers.

He snorted a couple of times & disappeared into the forest.

Later on down the road we got pictures of some bighorn sheep. We went to Lake Louise (which was on our way) to get a picture of the scenery there. The clouds were heavy over the mountains though & we didn't get our picture. Drove on to Radium Hot Springs & stopped there for a couple of hours. Went into the hot pool for about 45 minutes. It was like taking a big sauna bath.

We then went to the regular pool for a half hour or so. It was really welcome after not having a bath for 4 days. Drove on to the Wasa Lake Park Campground at Wasa, B.C. The mosquitoes were terrible here. B.C. is much like Louisiana except for the mountains. The grass is greener here than over the divide. It seems to rain more often, there are several swampy looking places, the underbrush is dense & there are plenty of mosquitoes. It rained a good bit of the night.

Tuesday 6/30/81

Drove to Cranbrook near Kimberly. In talking to government people we learn that we have a problem - we are not allowed to build a log cabin on government land. The only backcountry in B.C. all belongs to the Crown & none of it is for sale. Special permits are sometimes granted to build a permanent shelter in backcountry but this takes 6 months of red tape & we are told that our cause would probably not be granted. We go to Ron Shiber who's a customs official & wife is a hunting guide. (She has a guiding service with a Henry Fercho) I offer to build the cabin on his wife's hunting territory if he could obtain the permit to build it. When I leave, I would give him the

cabin to use as a spike camp. He seems agreeable but must clear this with the other partner & his wife & I must go to immigration to get permission as I am not allowed to work in Canada for any kind of compensation. Today Canada postal services go on strike - no mail moves & the length of the strike is undetermined. Tomorrow is Canada's birthday & everything closes down. We are not far from the border so we decide to go into Montana, mail our film & letters, check out the laws there in regards to building a log cabin & to see Glacier National Park. We can then decide whether to stay in Montana or come back to Cranbrook & pursue the matter with Ron Shiber. We cross the border & drive to Eureka, Montana. We learn also that backcountry land all belongs to the state or the US & is not for sale. However, we are advised that we may be able to obtain a recreational lease for a year that may allow us to build our log cabin. It is late & we must wait until tomorrow to check this out. We drive out of town & into the mountains to find a place to camp. We drove up a steep narrow logging road for about one and a half hours before we reached a flat spot on top of the mountain. We pitched the tent at 12 midnight. It rained all night.

Wednesday 7/1/81

We stayed in the tent most of the morning until the rain subsided. It was cold & wet. Drove down to Eureka only to learn that we must go to the Glacier View Ranger District to apply for a special use permit to build a log cabin the area. Drove down to Columbia Falls & called Ron Desjardine who is in charge of that ranger station (Glacier View). He did not think I would be granted a permit to build a permanent shelter even though I would burn it or tear it down when I left. I am to go to his office at 8:00 a.m. tomorrow to check the maps & talk further about my plans. We go to a motel, shower, eat & wash our clothes. I am becoming very frustrated & disheartened. Our social structure has become so tight that it does not even allow one to step outside of it. It is like a trap and allows no freedom from its escape. I only wish to live in the wilderness with nature for a year, to take pictures for all to see, and to do what my natural instincts drive me to do. I can see no harm in my desires, I do not wish to destroy anything in nature and it fact can be of help to the forest services, to wildlife agencies & to society in general. Even with the

offer to tear down the cabin & pack everything out, when I leave my request is denied. The officials feel that if they allow me to build a cabin then they must grant this to all who request it. But how many people ask to build a shelter for only a year in order to photograph wildlife. This seems indeed a special request, one which can be helpful, and certainly not one that would set grounds for the Forest Service of either the US or Canada to grant anyone permission to build a permanent shelter in the wilderness for and reason. I see an ever increasing lax in people to take responsibility to be assertive or get involved. It is far easier to say "no" than to say "yes" and risk even a measurable risk of having someone call them down for it. It's more comfortable and less effort just to say "no." All the reasons they give me to substantiate their denial either do not apply to me, or hold so little weight that they are not justifiable. I do not see how I can survive the winter in a tent (which is allowed) without a great deal of hardship. A tent does not sufficiently protect me from vandals, bears, the elements, etc. I must stock food for the entire winter & cannot store this in a tent because of the risk of bears eating it or even attacking me. The risk is too great as I will in all probability be snowed in and unable to obtain more food or help. My camera equipment, guns, and all other necessary equipment would be too great & easy a target for vandals. This could ruin my plans entirely. The problems are countless with a tent - I must have a more sturdy shelter. I must find a solution to this problem. If I cannot find a socially approved method, then I will find one suitable only to me. So many people say I should have lived a century ago - I certainly would not have encountered such problems as this. I

know of no one who loves & understands nature as I do. I will allow no man to infringe upon my right to live, and to live in my own way when I do no harm to him or his environment. Man has evolved himself away from nature to such an extent that he doesn't realize that his survival depends upon it, that he is indeed an inseparable part of it. He seems to even deny me the privilege of getting closer to it, & indeed helping him to know it better. I am damn frustrated with it all - don't know yet what I will do.

Thursday 7/2/81
We go down to the Montana Forest Service in Columbia Falls. They were expecting us. Not only was Ron Desjardine there, but he had with him his biologist, someone who helps set the hunting seasons, and a couple of others who did work in the Glacier View district. They brought maps, talked about where the game was when it was there, and what kind and amount was there.

They all seemed to want to help, but they did not allow me to build a more sturdy shelter. They themselves agreed that a tent was dangerous & not fit for the mountain winter. From the discussions I centered my interest on the North Fork of the Flathead River. To the North was Canadian Crown land, to the west, National Forest & to the East Glacier National Park. There was very little private land (held by people who homesteaded it many years ago). It was as far back into the wilderness as I could get in these

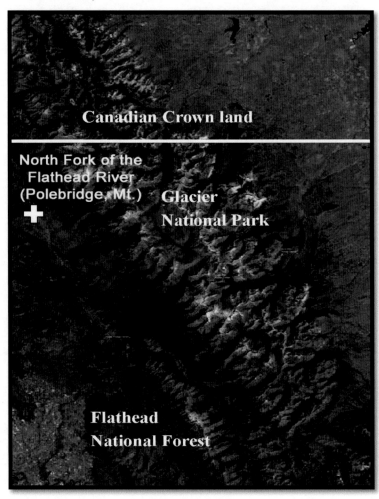

Old Homestead at Ann Hensen's

modern times. They directed me to George Ostrom who was an avid wildlife photographer, owned the Kalispell Weekly newspaper, and had land on the Canadian border. We drove to Kalispell and spoke to George. He said he could arrange to have me stay in one of his cabins on his land. He had American biologists (working on a bear tagging program with the Canadians) staying in one cabin and a girl he called "wolf girl" staying in another. She was studying wolves and would tag them and put sending units on them attached to a collar. We drove up the North Fork and inquired about land for sale. There was very little for sale and it seemed expensive for so remote a place. We went to the border and met one of the bear study team (don't know how many there were) and talked a while about what he does and where the bears were. Went over and met the "wolf girl" Diane Boyd. She was working on her thesis at the University of Montana. She was studying the habits of wolves and coyotes and had gained the title "wolf girl." We stayed in one of the cabins in "Moose Village" on the border.

The property

North Fork of the
Flathead River

Vance Hill

Polebridge Store

Friday 7/3/81

Drove back to a plot of land that was shown to us by Bob Olson. It overlooked the Flathead River and the big snowcapped mountains of Glacier Park. Talked to several of the residents in the area about land here. It seemed that no one knew of the plot (two acres) that we liked and felt that it was not for sale. Drove back to Columbia Falls to talk to the Forest Service people, to call my bank, and to see if Mac wanted to come in with me in buying the land. Banks were closed for 7/4 holidays. Mac wanted to discuss the proposition with his wife Joan – I was to call back at 10:00 p.m. When I called back Jane Mollett was there, was also interested in the land, and had several questions. Again they wanted time to think it over. I was to call back sometime around noon. Drove back up the North Fork and spent the night in the tent near the property.

Sat. 7/4/81

We were tired of driving around, talking to people and just getting frustrated. We went on the property we were planning to buy and cut firewood until 4:00 p.m. Went down to Hay Creek and took a bath. Went for a ride along the river in Glacier Nat. Park. Returned to Polebridge Mercantile store (about the only thing in Polebridge, Montana) to watch the locals shoot fireworks. Kevin slammed the truck door on his finger the other day and it has been bothering him considerably. Drove to a creek and spent the night in the tent.

Sun 7/5/81

Called Mac around noon. He and Jane agreed to buy one acre of land if I would buy the other. It would take all the money he had and I felt bad about that. Went to the property and marked off the road. Cut some dead trees on the roadway. Took pictures of the property for Mac to see. He was buying the land on my word only. Went for a dip in Hay Creek and drove to Columbia Falls. We were to see Charlotte Fischel about the land she had for sale and then to begin closing the sale if she didn't have something more attractive.

Mon. 7/6/81

Spent the morning talking to Charlotte Fischel about her land and making arrangements to close the sale of the property on the bluff. We were to buy this from Mr. Goodspeed from Maine. 1:00 p.m. Called Bob Olson in the North Fork who was to help us close the sale. He came in at 2:30 p.m. and went to Whitefish, Montana to see the bank officer (Schrieber) who handled the sale. Drove to Kalispell to get plot plans from courthouse there. Drove back to Columbia Falls and spent the night in the tent on the North Fork. It rained all night.

Tues 7/7/81

Went up to the Canadian border to talk to someone about hauling our logs for the log cabin. The timber on the property is too small for building a log cabin. Came back to the property and built a ramp for a bridge over the ditch so we could drive onto the property. It was muddy and rained all day. Our tent and sleeping bags were wet from the night before. And we were wet and muddy all over. Decided to go to Columbia Falls to sleep and pick up a chain to pull up the tree stumps that were in the driveway.

Charlotte Fischel's Outhouse

Wed. 7/8/81

Spent the morning getting groceries and supplies and talking to Forest Service people. Made arrangements to buy decking for the cabin floor from a small mill on the North Fork of the Flathead River. Spent the rest of the day cutting trees and pulling out stumps to make a road onto the property. Kevin lost his graduation ring in the process of building the road. Today the truck nearly fell

through the bridge. We had tied a chain from the truck to the stumps we were pulling out. The truck was on the bridge and Kevin was driving. The stump was so well rooted that the wheels began spinning on the log bridge and rolled the logs out from under the tires. The truck fortunately fell so that the tires were on the main supporting cross members. One of the logs flew out and got me on the shin. Luckily it didn't hit hard enough to break my leg. Finished about ½ the road today and set up the big tent for the first time. Something was fooling around the truck tonight.

Border Outhouse

Thurs.7/9/81
Worked on the road today until about 8:p.m., finished it. Went to the Hostel near Polebridge and learned that they had hot showers there for $1.00. Took a shower and came back to the tent. Something was fooling around the truck again tonight. Got up with the light but couldn't get a glimpse of it. It ran off about 50 yards into the woods. We have been told that a black bear frequently crosses our lot and we suspect it is trying to get the food in the truck.

Fri. 7/10/81
Cooked breakfast for the first time today. Noticed that a deer had walked down the road we built yesterday. Probably just checking it out to see if it approves. Kevin was pumping up the stove and I was looking for tracks that would indicate what has been trying to get into the truck for the last two nights. All of a sudden something big and black went crashing through the trees at an angle towards Kevin. I lit out a loud whistle and it stopped. I just stood there pointing so Kevin could look for it also. We never saw it again, but we both got a glimpse of it through the trees. It was either a moose or a black bear. Lots of things I like about this area, but 3 things come to mind; animals far outnumber people, there are no poisonous plants like poison ivy, oak, sumac etc., and there are no poisonous snakes. Today we worked on clearing the area where we are to build the cabin.

Photo By: James W Hale

Sat.7/11/81

We went down the road about 7 miles to pick out logs for the log cabin. The Dziuks who are neighbors went with us. As we are to buy the logs from Mr. Dziuk's employer. We stacked them so a hauler could just come in and just pick them up. Came back to the lot in late afternoon. And worked on clearing the area for the cabin

Sun. 7/12/81

Hauled gravel for the bridge approach today. Went up Hay Creek road and got 12 large flat rocks for our cabin foundation. Mac had left a message at the Pole Bridge store for me to call him back. He wanted to add Freddie Hebert's name as part owner of his lot. Will call the lawyer Mon. – hope it's not recorded yet. Washed the truck and took a bath in the creek. Built a tepee today to use for storage, and as a cook house until the cabin is built.

Mon 7/13/81

Spent the morning catching up on letter writing. Finished up the tepee and set up stove and cooking area inside. Put some supplies in the teepee. Cut trees and pulled stumps in the area around where cabin is to be built. Stacked out cabin and set first foundation rocks.

Tues. 7/14/81

Worked on setting the foundation rocks all day today. The Dziuk (pronounced Juk) kids have been coming by every day for an hour or so. They live a couple of blocks away. With the exception of one other, they are the only neighbors for miles. We have had a constant fire going for the last few days. We are burning the tree stumps only a couple at a time so as not to alert the fire look-out tower on Cyclone Mountain.

Wed. 7/15/81

We haven't heard the bear or whatever it was try to get into the truck for the last couple of nights. However, last night something big was breaking sticks and making a lot of noise in the woods next to the tent. Today we set more foundation rocks. Went up Hay Creek and got 3 more rocks to finish the foundation. These rocks weigh 500 pounds or so and put a load on the truck even with our beefed up overload springs. We finished setting the last of 18 foundation rocks today. It was a tough 2 days work as the ground is full of rocks and difficult to dig the holes for the foundation rocks. We use a small shovel and a crow bar for a pick. We went to the spring about a mile down the road and took a bath. It rained while we were taking a bath and it was cold. We came back to camp and I was standing by the fire eating a hot dog. Kevin was getting something out of the tepee. I noticed movement on the driveway behind the truck. At first I thought it was Kevin, But then I heard Kevin in the tepee. I looked again and there stood a beautiful white-tailed deer not more than 30 feet from me. In a calm voice I told Kevin to come out and look behind the truck. The deer just walked down the road right past us. I let out a low whistle and it stopped for a moment, then disappeared down the driveway in a fast walk.

Thurs. 7/16/81

Last night I was awakened by a hoofed animal as it bolted away from the tent door. Must have been a deer that came to investigate and picked up our scent or heard one of us snore? Woke up this morning and found deer tracks in the soft dirt all around us. They must swarm this place at night. Spent the morning writing and reading. Went up to the gravel hill (Vance Hill) and got 2 truckloads of gravel to put around the foundation rocks. All the Dziuk kids helped. Later that evening we went riding with all the Dziuk family to a lake up Cyclone Mountain Road. We saw a beautiful lake and a mule deer with 2

fawns. John David was trying to show me where to get a Tamarack (larch) tree, but we couldn't find a dead one near the road.

Friday 7-17-81
Went up Moose Creek Road & found a large Tamarack tree. Cut three 7' lengths out of it and brought them to camp. Drove to Columbia Falls to get supplies & take care of some business. Went to see about getting the snowmobile and Kevin's airplane ticket & we washed our clothes.

Outhouse off Moose creak road on left a couple of miles down

Saturday 7-18-81
Went back up Moose Creek Rd. & to Center Mountain Rd. & found another Tamarack tree. Cut another 3 lengths 7 ft. long & brought them to camp. Went to Polebridge store & played volleyball in the rain with a group of the local people. As another storm came in about dark everyone jumped in their trucks before it got to us. As we were driving back to camp it began hailing so hard it was deafening inside the truck cab. By the time we got to camp (2.5 miles) the ground was covered with hail. About 1 hour later as we were eating, Kevin remembered that he had laid his watch on the truck hood while we were playing volleyball. We drove back & luckily found the watch on the road. The crystal was broken, but it hadn't been run over

Sunday 7-19-81

Worked all day on putting up the foundation pillows that we cut out of the Tamarack logs. We got half of them up. We couldn't use one of them because a beetle had gotten into it and we were afraid this would cause the wood to rot easier. Tomorrow we will get another. As I was cooking that night in the tepee, Kevin was reading in the tent. When he came out to eat, a deer was sniffing the pole that holds up the tent flap, and they both scared each other. A buck was also nearby & neither was too frightened as we watched them for a while. A few minutes later Kevin goes to get some bread out of the back of the truck and nearly walks into another deer. Again they both scared each other.

Monday 7-20-81

Looked all day for another Tamarack tree. Ended up cutting a live one. It was a frustrating, rainy, tiring day. It seemed like a waste to work so hard all day just to locate & cut one tree.

10 miles North of Polebridge

Tuesday 7-21-81

Went to Polebridge store to get mail & make phone calls. Came back to camp & worked on setting the pilings (pillars) for the cabin. We finally cut them all and by dark had only 2 of them left to level. Took some pictures of a spike buck that was walking around the woodpile. As I was eating my supper in the tepee I heard a deep low grunt. Kevin had finished eating & was in the tent about 20 feet away. I thought he had made some noise. A few minutes the same again. The third time, I called to Kevin to ask if he had made any noise. He said "no." Today a man in Glacier Park only 15 miles from here had been attacked by a Grizzly. I thought that if a bear was out there & came walking into the tepee to get some food, the only way out for me was the same way he came in. I picked up a hatchet and went out to see what was out there. I saw nothing. Got the gun out of the truck & finished eating my supper with it next to me.

59

Wed. 7/22/81

Finished leveling the foundation pillars. Coated them with penta and diesel oil to prevent rot. Began cutting our logs and peeling the bark off of them. Heard something, probably a moose tramping through a marshy area as we went to get another log at the end of the driveway. I ran to get the camera, but couldn't find it (the moose). We really got dirty today, so we went down to the Hostel for a shower. The owner was going to take casts of some big mountain lion tracks just behind the Hostel. Kevin went to play cards at the Dziuk's house. I went to camp to eat and go to bed.

Thurs. 7/23/81

Worked on putting up the main supporting sills. Got three of the four of them up. It rained on and off all day today and the work wasn't pleasant.

Fri.7/24/81

Went to the Polebridge Mercantile to get our mail and make some phone calls. Every so often I get a strange feeling as though my subconscious is picking up some sort of signal or communication. Sometimes this feeling is blissful, sometimes very saddening and distracting. About a week ago I felt to a moderate sense that I was picking up some sort of signal as though I had suffered some sort of loss. Today, to a great extent, I felt as though something was telling me I have suffered a great loss not yet known to me. I was so distracted and felt so bad that I Completed only the one sill left today. I am not sure what is going on, but it is very saddening. Perhaps this has something to do with it – or perhaps it has something to do with my girlfriend, Pat Saedlo. We have been communicating by phone and by mail quite regularly, and to all outward appearances, all seems well. However about two weeks before I left, something was running through her mind and several times I found that she was in her room with the door locked (an unusual behavior for her). I haven't heard from her in a week now and I miss her very much. Well, whatever it is, it will show up sooner or later. On the way back from Polebridge we got several shots of 5 deer near the camp. Later on during the

evening they came back. We took more pictures and fed them peanuts. We played with them for about 3 hours. They seem to be getting used to us and are not afraid. We got to where we could approach within 10 or 12 feet of them. After a while another buck showed up and would scrap with the only other buck in the herd. It was the first time I have seen 2 deer stand up on their hind feet and swing at each other as though boxing. Kevin's friends haven't been writing to him and he seems more hurt today than usual that he didn't get any mail from home. Went down to Polebridge to call Pat. It was 11:00 p.m. in Philadelphia and she wasn't home. Talked to Kim awhile. Received my pictures from Mrs. Hurst today. Was rather upset that the negatives seemed to be scratched up considerably, and in talking to Mrs. Hurst earlier this week she said some of the negatives had been folded. I called Pierre at Dixiecolor lab about it today. Two days ago I hurt my back picking up some heavy poles above my head. Kevin will be leaving on the 19th and I am concerned that the cabin may not be where I can handle it by then – not much time left.

Sat. 7/25/81

Worked on putting up the floor joists today. We cut and shaved 9 of 11 of them. Tomorrow we hope to cut the last 2 and then notch them into place. The left front disc brake on the truck was making noise today. It appears as though the brake pads are gone. I replaced these just before we left– didn't seem to last very long. Our friends the deer came back today about 7:30 p.m. We are making friends with them quite rapidly. They (6 of them) walked all through our construction work. And ate peanuts which we trew to them. They came much closer today, perhaps within 5 feet or so of us. Soon we should have them eating out of our hands. They see few people out here and seem not to be afraid of us, only curious. We are now able to distinguish between them and have named 4 of them, "Peanuts" for the little light colored one, "Smokey" for the dark faced one, "Sparkey" for the little buck, and "Scratch" for the one with the scar on his side. We went to the Polebridge store to get some food as we were running low. One of the swift's mud nests had fallen from under the roof. A young swift was knocked out of the nest – too young

to make it on his own. We took it to camp and will try to feed it until it can fly. Also last night the deer came around camp and played and cut up most of the night. They were not quiet as they had been.

Sun. 7/26/81

Today goes down as a very sad day. Kevin has been dragging and going around with a don't care attitude. We were dragging logs with the truck. Kevin was driving and I was hooking the chain to the logs. He didn't hold the brake well and the truck backed up. Now I had to say something or else one of us would get hurt. We could be caught between a log and the truck, or he could pull up as I was hooking the chain and snap off a finger or any number of other accidents. I asked him to get out of the truck and tell me what was wrong. He said he didn't want to spend his summer making a log cabin. He wanted to play on the snow, in the lakes etc. He said he hadn't wanted to drive all over to see the country as we did. We had a discussion about it. His

attitude was poor, he thought of other things he could be doing instead. I didn't believe all he said, as I know he did enjoy most of the trip and did expect to build a log cabin. Most kids would trade places with him on the spot. I figured he was bored and had difficulty sticking to the work. I didn't know how I would complete the cabin alone, but nothing would be worse losing favor with my only son. I told him, I didn't want him here if he really didn't want to be here. I would arrange plane fare back home by Tuesday. I sat in the tepee for an hour and then went down the side of the mountain and cried it out. Went for a walk down to the river and returned to camp a couple of hours later. Asked Kevin to go do something else and to leave me alone for a while. I worked on the cabin with no desire for the rest of the afternoon. Kevin came back to camp at 1:45 a.m. The big buck came to camp that night and played around the tent. I finally went to sleep around 4am feeling very sad about everything.

Mon. 7/27/81

Had a long talk with Kevin. He didn't want to go home. He had said things he didn't mean. And I apologized for fussing at him about the driving. We mended things and tried to better understand each other's needs and the situation we were in. I felt a lot of it was the adjustment we had to make living out here – rather drastic to what we were used to. Worked on the cabin the rest of the day. Kevin wanted to bring the truck by the cabin to play the radio. I had no objections.

There is more strength in understanding than in all the world's riches.
James Hale

Tues. 7/28/81

The radio stayed on all day today. I realized that I made a mistake by not letting Kevin bring his radio. He seems to need this. We worked on notching the floor joists into place (my job) and peeling logs (Kevin's job). The Dziuks went to Columbia Falls today to shop and brought back some brake pads for the truck.

Wed. 7/29/81
We worked all day on notching floor joists and peeling logs. This part of the cabin is slow – a lot of notching on each log.

Thurs. 7/30/81
Changed the brake pads on the truck. Went to Columbia Falls and Kalispell. Bought rope for pulling up the logs. Bought groceries, washed cloths, bought salt blocks for animals and a bag of feed for the deer. I also bought an Arctic cat (Pantera) snowmobile. The dealer will hold it until first snow or until I get the cabin built. I bought rods for wall reinforcement. Stopped by Lee Downes' place to see if he had our floor boards cut and if he had a metal detector to help locate Kevin's ring.

Fri. 7/31/81

Worked all day on notching the first wall log to the floor joist. This is probably the most tedious log to fit on the cabin. I felt bad mentally all day.

Sat. 8/1/81

Woke up at 8 a.m. and went to Columbia Falls to spend the day at their Heritage Festival. Saw a parade, handwork stands, listened to a band, watched the various local Fire Depts. Compete in games & went to a rodeo and later that night a street dance. The Fireman's games were the most enjoyable for me. Kevin played with his "yampee" puppet everywhere we went and it was the center of attention. We laughed all day at peoples' reactions. The best of all is when we walked in a bar and sat next to an old drunk. The yampee sat there, drank beer, ate popcorn and put on a show for the drunk. He just couldn't believe it and still thought it was real when we left. He'll be talking about that for a long time. We got home around midnight.

Sun. 8/2/81

Got up late and worked on the cabin – finished fitting the 1st wall log. Felt bad mentally about Pat. Went to Polebridge store at 8:00 and called Pat. We talked about an hour or more. She seems to be very distant from me & I feel she is pulling away. There was nothing in the conversation that I could feel good about. It feels to me as though the end of our relationship is near. Came home and went right to bed - didn't feel like eating – my stomach was burning and I felt cold. Didn't sleep at all this night

Mon 8/3/81

At daylight I began writing a letter to Pat. It was mid or late afternoon (don't even know) when I finished gathering my thoughts & finished the letter. Got something to eat (hadn't eaten since noon yesterday) and worked on the cabin the rest of the day. Was very lacking in will today.

Tues. 8/4/81
Went to Polebridge store to mail letter to Pat, Freddie Hebert, and sent films to Mrs. Hurst, and a Polebridge t-shirt to Lisa for her birthday tomorrow. Worked on fitting the first wall log on the other side of the cabin. Didn't quite finish it today.

Wed. 8/5/81
Called Lisa this morning & wished her a Happy Birthday. Didn't have much for a gift, but bought her a Polebridge, Mt. T-shirt and mailed it to her in yesterday's mail. We began putting up the wall logs today. Glad to get off the foundation. It looks like we made some progress today. Should move faster now, show-wise. Kevin worked on making a raft for us to float down the North Fork of the Flathead River.

Thurs. 8/6/81

Kevin finished his raft today. I put up 1 row of logs on the cabin. It was hot and my get up and go just couldn't get up and go today. We drink 2 gallons of water on days like this, 90°. Hot and dry.

Fri. 8/7/81

Went for mail today and to call Helen. Couldn't reach her. About 2:00 p.m. the lady from the Polebridge store came over to camp to tell us that Kevin's grandfather had died (Helen had called her) We didn't know who (which grandfather), and went to call Helen. Took 45 minutes or so to get through. Lyes Bourg had died of a massive heart attack. We worked on the cabin the rest of the day, only got up 3 logs.

Sat. 8/8/81

Today we took the day off of work for some enjoyment. We learned the water was too shallow in places to float Kevin's raft, so we decided to try again to find a rubber one to rent. We drove through Glacier Park & to the little town of Apgar, a neat little place. We rented bicycles here and rode through a little

trail through the woods and on to West Glacier. Here we found a swimming hole around an abandoned bridge. We swam there (the middle fork of the Flathead River) for about an hour. We had fun jumping off the bridge (37' above the water) and swinging off the bridge from a rope. Kevin wrecked the bicycle 3 times – driving too reckless. Twice we had to bend the frame back in place so it could be ridden again. We drove to Bowman Lake Via. a narrow park road. Here we could float our raft on another day. We went by to visit Ron Fisher, a neighbor on the ridge behind us.

Sun. 8/9/81
We worked on the cabin all day. The weather was a hot and dry 90°. Progress was slow – only 3 logs today. Went to the hostel for a shower & then to Bill Brown's (neighbor at the end of the road) for a visit. We planned a float trip with them for Wed. I called Pat - not home

Mon. 8/10/81
Worked on the cabin all day today. Felt very strange today - couldn't put my finger on it. A sad feeling. Then at about 7:30 p.m. Karen Feather who owns the Polebridge store came over to the

place. I knew something must be wrong otherwise she wouldn't have come. On 8/7/81 her mother had come bearing bad news of Mr. Bourg's death. She said that my mother had called and for me to return the call – it was urgent. I thought my Dad must be very ill and back in the hospital. I blocked out everything worse. I was concerned though. For several weeks I have been feeling very disturbed inside, as though I was to suffer a great loss of some kind. Some kind of signal – don't know what it is though. I have been having serious problems with my relationship with Pat Losing her would be a great loss to me – especially now. I have been tuned in to this problem. We went to the Polebridge store & called my Mom. She said that Dad had died. I didn't want to believe this, and asked her again to verify what I had heard. God! This was heavy. What greater loss can one have than to lose one of his parents? I had to ask Mom (Gene) to hold on a minute before I was able to talk again. She told me he had one of his asthma spells and didn't pull out of it. We went back to the camp, packed a few things, put up the tools and went to the airport in Kalispell, Mt. We arranged a flight to leave for Baton Rouge, La at 5:15 am tomorrow morning. Mrs. Hurst was to pick us up at 4:40 p.m. in Baton Rouge. David and Alice, and Dot and Harold were to be in New Iberia tonight. Dot's daughter Ruth was with Mom – I'm thankful someone was with her. We went to a motel in Kalispell.

Widney & Gene Hale

Tues. 8/11/81

I couldn't sleep at all – things kept going through my mind. I kept trying to make better contact with the signals (feeling of some kind) I had been getting for the last few weeks. They have been very strong, upsetting and very real, but I can't get close enough contact to understand them. I will keep trying. These feelings seem to be a powerful communication of some kind, and for reaching. They seem to come from inside somewhere as though they are somehow communicating with all things that effect or control me. Perhaps it is some sort of inborn, subconscious, communication that has been developed through the evolutionary process. Whatever it is, there must be some signs somewhere that would help me to better understand it. At 4:00am I got up and went out to find a box. I wrapped my gun case with the cardboard and tied it with string. Another couple in the hotel was going to the airport and were on the same flight as we were. They rode with us. We had 4 plane changes to get to Baton Rouge, La. The air traffic controllers were on strike and many flights were canceled or altered. The airplane stayed on the ground in Denver, Colorado ½ hour overtime and we missed our connecting flight in Dallas. We couldn't get another flight for 3 hours. Called Mrs. Hurst in Baton Rouge (at the airport) to tell her of our problem. She waited for us for 3 hours. We arrived in Lafayette about 10:00 p.m. I hadn't slept and was sort of dizzy. I called Mom earlier at the funeral home. She said that it would close at 10:00 p.m. I didn't want to drive, and didn't want to keep her up waiting for me, and the house was full of people. I stayed at the Hurst's this night, took Kevin home.

Wed. 8/12/81
Went to New Iberia about 8:30 a.m. In the Hurst's truck. The Funeral was 2:00 p.m., all seemed to go well, but I had difficulty in controlling my feelings – a sad day. At 4:00 p.m. Mrs. Land and a friend from the Methodist church brought several platters of food that the church members had cooked. Mrs. Hurst had cooked a huge ham and a gallon of crawfish etouffee.

Everyone seemed so nice and helpful. Dot and her family, and John and Velma Rosser, and Lois Finch slept at the house. David Alice and I went to sleep at Robert Mc Jimsey's house. I called Pat in Pa. at 10:00 p.m.

Photo of the Hale House

Tues 8/13/81

Took care of finances etc. and got my 9mm pistol at Mac's. I took Mom to Social Security Office, bank, Internal Revenue, and began taking care of final business. It appears we will have approximately $20,000 in outstanding debts. But have not seen the mortgage certificate and may have other debts. Dad did not let anyone in on what he owed or what business he was conducting. John and Velma went home today. Harold's uncle died and he had to leave to go to that funeral. They were to return on Saturday. Larry Hurst called today and said he could use the Mexican boys in his restaurant (working for Dad). We talked to them today and they agreed to go to the restaurant tomorrow to talk to Mr. Hurst. I will pick them up at 1:00 p.m. tomorrow.

Fri. 8/14/81

Went to Lafayette to take care of any insurance business I might have, and to visit with my friends there. I went to Hub City Bank to take care of Dad's business there. The note he had there will be taken care of by insurance. This will save us about $9,000. Phil Noris wanted me to go by Wednesday night to visit. Went to Riverside Inn and called my mother to bring the Mexican boys over – I was running late. She did and they accepted the job. They will begin working tomorrow. We had Sally (one of the waitresses who spoke Spanish) interpret for us. They told the account about what happened to Dad at the job. It seems he mixed muriatic acid & clorox together and got a vigorous reaction. He was close to the 5 gal. bucket where the chemicals were mixed and breathed the gases that were given off. He immediately began coughing and motioned the Mexican boys away. He coughed so much that his face turned red. He had a bottle of spray in his pocket that he kept in case of an asthma attack. He used the spray, but it didn't seem to help. He ran to his truck without saying a word & hurried off. He drove to his house across the highway, jumped out of the truck without even closing the door,

and ran into the house. He asked Mom to quickly give him 2 of his cortisone pills that he takes for asthma. She had some right on the counter and immediately gave them to him. He swallowed them with water, threw his head back and quit breathing. Mom said it seemed like he had severe muscle spasms. Ruth Martin was there & she and Mom tried to get him on the floor to give him artificial respiration. He was too heavy for them. They got help from someone in the trailer park & then called an ambulance. CPR didn't seem to work, and when the ambulance arrived, the medic couldn't get the hose down his throat to give him oxygen. It was as though his bronchial tubes were closed tight. The air seemed only to go in his

78

stomach. They rushed him to the hospital, working on him all the time. He never recovered, and was pronounced dead at the hospital. I called Don Weintritt at his lab and he said the main reaction gave off large amounts of free chlorine gas. Until today we thought Dad had died of a severe asthma attack. Mom did suspect something else though, as he died rather quickly – not his usual asthma attack that came on much slower. We asked the Mexican boys to write down the account in case we would need it. The death certificate shows his death as a cardiopulmonary arrest set off by an asthma attack. We will now have to have this changed. This could be especially important to Mom if he has Workman's Comp. benefits or group life insurance. Otherwise there would be no need to change it – He is dead no matter how it happened and nothing can bring him back.

Sat. 8/15/81

Went around the place to try and sum up what needed to be done & in what order. I put aside some things to bring to Montana if I would go back. David and Alice have tentative plans to go up Labor Day weekend. If they do go,

and I also, then perhaps they can take a few things with them. It seems that Mom should keep most of the tools etc. but perhaps can sell some of the trailers, extra power saws etc. that she won't need. The Mexican boys began work at the Riverside Inn today. We will lease or rent the truck to them so they will have transportation. This will solve the problem of what they will do for a living. They will also be there to help Mom cut grass & keep up the place. It will also keep the truck around in case Mom needs it. Thanks to the Hurst's for employing them. Hope the boys will be helpful to them & to Mom also. It seems like a very workable solution. We will need to get one a driver's license though – none of them have a license. But Adan has previously owned a car & knows how to drive. We also need to get insurance on him & have him sign a rental – lease agreement. I slept at Mac's house in my own bed. Mom's house is full.

81

Sun 8/16/81

David, Alice, Mom's sister Lois, and Kevin left today. Kevin will spend a few days with David and Alice before school starts. I went to visit the Hurst's until about 5:30 p.m. I met Joan McJimsey and Joan Mollett at my old apartment & swam for a while. I called Phil Noris; I will go to his house Wed. for a visit. Slept at Mac's.

Mon 8/17/81

Went through the papers in the office & set up some files of my own so I would have a system to get through the problems to come. I went to Lafayette to find a lease agreement & to take care of some of Dad's business. Mom had gotten statements from the Mexican boys about what happened to Dad on the job. She brought them to Dad's Spanish teacher for translation. I made copies and took them to the coroner, Dr. Musso as he would need them to correct the death cert. Dad's doctor, Dr. Alvarez will help us with any translations etc. Neither the Coroner nor Dr. Alvarez attended Dad at his death. I slept at Mac's tonight.

Tues 8/18/81

I went to the New Iberia courthouse to check out the mortgage certificate on Dad's property & the liens against it. Went to Building and Loan to take care of accounts and Dad's other business that he may have had. Joe Boudreaux of Dad's employer (Show Construction Co.) came to the house today. We gave him a working time for the Mexican boys & Dad. We spoke to him about what happened to Dad & asked that he check to see if Dad had any group insurance. Also told him we would be sending him paper work to file a workman's comp. claim. He said Dad was working by the hour and this would confirm that he was covered by workman's comp. I slept at Mac's tonight.

Wed. 8/19/81

Today Mom, Adan, and Dot left at 6:00a.m. to go to Texas so Adan can take his driving test & get a license. Louisiana does not give the test in Spanish. And he doesn't know enough English to take the test. I spent the day talking to creditors and trying to settle some of Dad's accounts. Then went to Phil & Barbara Norse's for dinner (supper). Rodney & Darlene Savoi were there also. It was Willie & Delores East's anniversary and they couldn't be there. I enjoyed seeing them and had a great visit. I slept at Mac's house. Mom is still in Texas.

Thurs. 8/20/81

I helped Mac's Dad hang curtains at Mac's house this morning. I went to Iberia savings and loan to close out a small savings account & check out a mortgage note. Closed out another small savings account at First Federal Savings & Loan. Don't know why Dad had such small amounts (under $20) in these accounts for so many years. I went to New Iberia National Bank to check out an old mortgage note that was still against the property since 1961,

I think, Bank has no records of it. I tried to cancel the note at the Courthouse, but was unable to do it – need some paperwork. I went to Lafayette to open new accounts so Mom wouldn't have to keep a lot of money in the house & so creditors couldn't seize it – put them in my name. I worked at Metropolitan office for a while & called some of Dad's creditors in the area. Spoke to R.J. Shaw today about Dad's pay roll, his hourly pay, etc. He said Dad was working by the hour. This should confirm that Dad would be covered for workman's comp. benefits. I

Robert Mc Jimsey (Mac)

told him I would send paperwork to file a claim. I recorded the conversation on tape. Mom came back at 7:30 p.m., just as I got to the house. Jose Adan Martinez had finally gotten his driver's license. They had run into problems and were gone for two days. This solves another problem – now we can lease him the truck so he can go to work. I can probably return to Montana to finish my log cabin & Mom can come for the trip. Mom and I were to go out to Toby's with the Hurst's at 8:00 p.m. The whole family was there as well as some guests. We had a great meal and good company. Mom enjoyed it but was so tired. We got home around midnight. Dot and Harold had ben chauffeuring the Mexicans to the Riverside Inn ever since they began work. I slept at Mac's house.

Fri. 8/21/81

I talked to Mom this morning from Mac's house about what we needed to do today. She began crying and said she was so tired. She doesn't sleep well at night. I went straight home and helped her with paying the bills and getting things straight so we could head for Montana on Sunday. She calmed down and things went well for a day. Dot, Harold and their family left today to go back home. I went to Lafayette to the Hub City Bank to cancel Dad's Hale Construction Co. account and check on the loan account. Then I went to Nugies Insurance agcy. to get insurance for Adan. Then to Metropolitan to get insurance for Mom and to show a client my wildlife pictures; as he wanted to buy some. Mom went to New Iberia to close her personal savings account, to renew her driver's license, and to Broussard to deposit the money into the new account at Hub City Bank. Mom and I went to Mr. McJimsey's house for a seafood dinner at 6:00 p.m. I slept at Mom's house tonight.

Sat. 8/22/81

I went to New Iberia to balance the front tires on the truck, back home to change the oil, adjust clutch, fix squeak on speedometer cable & generally check out the truck before turning it over to Adan. I had Adan sign for his insurance and the lease, had Mom sign for her insurance. Then went to Lafayette to mail Adan's insurance application, to Metropolitan to bring Mom's Insurance app. Then drove to Kaplan to pick up Freddie's chain block, as I will use it in Montana to lift the logs. Talked to Ella May and Freddie for a while then went back to the Hurst's to pick up some cases of fruit I had them get for me, as well as my guns and camera lens. Bided them good bye. Went home and with the help of Adan and Jesus we covered the foundation of the little house Dad had begun. Gathered some of the things I was to bring to Montana. Slept at Mom's. Since Dad died on 8/10/81. I have not stopped pushing – there has been no idle time. Perhaps tomorrow as we start the trip back to Montana, we can all relax a little. I bring with me some unfinished business, as well as files I need to follow up on things I have been doing with Dad's business. I slept at Mom's tonight.

Sun 8/23/81

We decided to go in Mom's car. It was noon before we got the car checked out and everything packed and loaded. We picked Helen up and left Lafayette about 1:00 p.m. We arrived at David's house in Dallas, Texas at about 10:00 p.m. All day today I had a sad feeling inside. Mom told me later that evening that today is Dad's birthday. I wasn't able to sleep and went outside and walked around awhile, finally got to sleep at about 1:00 a.m.

Mon 8/24/81

We left David & Alice's at 8:00 a.m. We arrived in Pueblo, New Mexico about 10:30 p.m. All seems to be going OK.

Tues 8/25/81

We left pueblo at 8:00 a.m., went to Royal Gorge and the cowboy old west town of Buckskin Joe. We left there about 1:00 p.m. arrived in Lander, Wyoming about 11:30 p.m.

8/26/81

Left about 10 a.m., and drove to Yellowstone Nat. Park. I took some pictures of elk and looked around the park. We arrived at Bozeman, Mt at 10:00 p.m. Helen brought to my attention that Dad died on the 10th of August, the very day in 1969 that I jumped off an oil platform in the Gulf of Mexico to save her and ended up fighting so hard for 18 hours to save my own life.

JAMES HALE and wife, Helen, are pictured a-
bove, with the outboard that almost cost him his
life Sunday night. The only evidence of his 17-hour
ordeal in the Gulf of Mexico waters was the cushion strap marks above his armpits.   (Staff Photo)

The following was written by James Hale
Followed by newspaper article

The waters were calm. The sun was just beginning to peak over the morning horizon. Twenty-eight-year-old James W. Hale, his wife Helen, and his sister-in-law, Nina Dupuy, pulled their little outboard alongside an unoccupied drilling platform some ten miles off the coast of Grand Isle, Louisiana. Anticipating a beautiful day for fishing and sunbathing, the three eagerly unloaded their fishing gear onto the platform.

The warm August day began like any ordinary day; but as it wore on, the winds steadily increased, becoming unusually brisk by twelve noon. The seas were yanking fairly hard on the boat's bowline, and Hale became concerned that it might break and set their boat adrift. As a precaution, he secured the boat with a second line. By mid afternoon the sky had become very hazy, the winds much higher than usual, and the seas nearly four feet. Little did the party know that Camille, one of the most devastating hurricanes ever to lash the shores of the Gulf of Mexico, was gathering winds and brewing its mighty force far out at sea. By seven o'clock the air had turned cold, and the seas were cresting well over six feet. There was no sign of the usual late afternoon slack in the winds.

Time was running out, and the trio decided not to wait any longer. Helen got into the boat, and untied one of the bowlines, as it was needed to transfer the fishing gear from the platform to the bobbing boat. Then the inevitable happened. A heavy wave slammed into the boat, breaking the other bowline and setting the boat adrift. Hale, with unmistakable concern in his voice, yelled instructions to his wife to start the engine. Although the electric starter cranked continually, the cold engine would not kick over. As fate would have it, the battery ran down before the engine could be primed and started. The boat, now nearly three hundred yards off the platform, was drifting fast in the rough seas. Helen looked to her husband for help.

93

Hale's mind began to race! The seas were getting rougher and would soon begin to break. How long could the little boat stay afloat? Since nightfall was rapidly approaching, the chances of his wife being spotted this far out were rather slim. He knew he could start the engine with the manual starter and drive back to the platform - if he could get to the boat. But could he catch the boat, drifting as fast as it was? Deeply fearful for his wife's safety, he felt he had no other choice. He turned to his sister-in-law and said, "I've got to try for it". She pleaded with him not to go as he grabbed a floatation cushion and jumped into the water. Hale was a good swimmer in excellent physical condition. He struck out at a hard steady pace, but soon realized that he was in more trouble than he had bargained for. He was caught in a swift outgoing tide that pulled him away from the wind-driven boat. In a desperate attempt to close the gap, he began swimming at nearly full pace. The cushion was holding him back; he was rapidly burning up energy. Though he thought several times of letting it go, he held on to it. Helen tried to check the boat's drift by paddling, but the rough seas rendered her efforts futile. The struggle lasted for several minutes before Hale became exhausted, and settled down to catch his breath. His heart sank as he watched his wife drift away like a bobbing cork in the endless sea.

It was nearly a half mile back to the platform when he turned to swim back. But the tide was against him, it allowed him no time to rest, and he had spent his energy. Nina, alone on the platform, watched helplessly as her two companions disappeared into the impending darkness.

Hale, now concentrating on his own survival, tried to keep calm by singing and talking to himself. Then he thought - Sharks! (The gulf waters are the domain of many species of sharks, the most vicious and unpredictable fish in the sea.) As a scuba diver, Hale had learned that sharks attack mostly near the

surface. He hoped that the rough seas would keep them in deeper water. Trying
the floatation cushion in every position imaginable, he found that, in the
rough water, it was most helpful in the position the label cautioned against –
on the back. After an hour or so in the cool water, chills set in, and Hale
began to tremble all over. The chills gradually gave way to a tingling feeling.
He began to feel numb and weak as the energy was slowly being drained from his
body.

As the tides carried him out to sea, he drifted within sight of several
oil platforms marked by small blinking lights, visible for seven or eight
miles. Singling out one of the platforms, he estimated his drift and struck
out on a course that would take him to it. But before he could reach it, the
tides or the winds would change direction, throwing him far off course.
Repeated attempts were unsuccessful and used up precious energy.

Hale was startled by a loud clap of thunder, rolling through the night
air. He turned and encountered a cloud blacker than the night, rapidly
approaching from the north. Soon he was surrounded by the cracking of light-
ning and the roar of thunder. The high winds drove the cold rain stinging
onto his face and whipped the seas to powerful ten-foot breakers that would
pick him up, and on each crest, tumble him under water. When he surfaced, he
had only time enough to take a breath before being tumbled by the next crest.
Several times during the storm the floatation cushion was ripped from his back,
compounding the difficulty of his plight. Sheer stamina and a strong will to
live kept him fighting one wave after another until the storm began to subside.
It had been a bad storm, pushing him several miles farther out to sea, and
leaving him completely exhausted.

Meantime, a large fishing vessel from Biloxi, Mississippi, changed course
to investigate a flashing light in the open sea. It was Helen. She was taken

aboard and given the best of care. Fortunately, she recalled the number of the platform and its position was located on the map. After two hours of plowing through the heavy seas, the big boat finally reached the platform. Nina, freezing in her bathing suit, had to swim to the boat as the seas were too rough for the craft to approach the structure. When Helen learned that her husband had not make it back to the platform, she became gravely concerned. The captain immediately radioed the U.S. Coast Guard at Grand Isle, Louisiana. The seas were too rough for the local boats, and the Coast Guard cutter Point Lookout was dispatched out of Morgan City, Louisiana. It arrived on the scene about three o'clock, and joined the fishing vessel in a difficult search of the area.

Far out at sea, Hale saw the powerful searchlights as little streaks on the horizon. He was kicking at a much slower pace now, just enough to keep afloat. His whole body was numb; his hands and feet were nearly void of feeling. The salt water had blurred his vision, his voice was almost gone, and his hearing was dulled. The fate of his wife weighed heavily on his mind. It was just before daylight when another clap of thunder rolled through the sky. Another storm! This one out of the south. Hale took off his bathing suit, tore it into strips, and tied the floatation cushion to his back. Much weaker now, his chances of survival looked dim as the raging storm began to whip up the seas. The fury of this storm was no less than the first, but the strong-willed Hale fought on until the storm passed. It drove him miles closer to shore, leaving him almost paralyzed. As daybreak came, he was disturbed to see that his hands and feet were blue, and the area between his toes and fingers a deep purple. The straps from the cushion had worn through the skin, causing his shoulders to bleed.

Meanwhile, back on Grand Isle, a full scale search was getting underway.

Coast Guard heliocopters rose into the air and headed for the open sea. Radio signals went out to all boats and aircraft in the area to be on the lookout. Two oil company heliocopters volunteered to join in the search. Mrs. Hale made every effort to rally help. Two boats were lost in the stormy seas that night, and the boat captains were unwilling to leave safe harbor. A friend attempted to fly a small plane to Grand Isle to help in the search, but was forced to turn back because of bad weather. There was much doubt that Hale would be found alive, but neither his wife nor the Coast Guard was ready to give up hope.

Some fifteen miles offshore, Hale's spirits lifted as he spotted one of the heliocopters moving back and forth in its search pattern. It was only a speck on the early morning horizon, but it was getting closer and closer to his position. He untied the floatation cushion and began waving it anxiously. The chopper came within a half mile of him before turning back and heading in to shore. He had not been spotted.

It was about mid-day when Hale spotted smoke on the horizon. As it drew into the range of his blurred vision, he realized it was coming from the exhaust of a large shrimping boat. Water sprayed high over the bow as the boat plowed through the heavy seas. It listed heavily, nearly dipping its outriggers into the water. Its course was a little off to one side, and Hale swam to position himself directly in its line of travel. With high hopes, he began yelling and waving excitedly. As it approached, it didn't slow down, and was almost on top of him when he realized it wasn't going to stop. He swam in a desperate attempt to clear the keel, and at the last instant turned to kick the bow in hopes of pushing away from it. It was too late - the bow struck him a hard blow, knocking the wind out of him and forcing him beneath the hull. Hale was certain that his number was up, but at least it would be over quickly. The water twisted and tumbled him beneath the boat. The time seemed like an eternity as he waited for the propellors to strike him. Instants later he came bobbing up in the propwash behind the boat. The propellors had miraculously missed him. Gasping for breath, the frustrated but fortunate Hale watched the seemingly unoccupied shrimper heading out to sea. Alas! again, he hadn't been seen.

The storms had tested his endurance to the limit. His several attempts to reach the platforms had left him weak and discouraged. His chances of being spotted looked hopeless. He had been fighting heavy seas for eighteen hours and was near the point of losing consciousness. Now he was run over by a boat. What kind of torture did the sea yet have in store for him?

Hale hadn't seen the heliocopters since early that morning, and assumed they had given up the search. As he spotted another platform in the distance, he said out loud, "I'll never give up". Swimming toward the platform, he was startled by a loud roaring noise from above. He looked up to behold a large red and white Coast Guard heliocopter dropping down to his position. Red lights were flashing. Radio signals were being sent out in all directions. Hale had been found! The pilot tried to set down the heliocopter, but the craft was slapped back into the air by the rough seas. The Coast Guard cutter Point Lookout was in the area, and the heliocopter pilot had radioed for help. The cutter chopped through the heavy seas at nearly full throttle and was on the scene within a few minutes. The captain cautiously kept the big boat well away from Hale to keep the seas from pounding him against the hull. A rope ladder was thrown down the side, and Hale was helped to the deck. He was wrapped in a blanket, put into a rescue basket, and hoisted up to the hovering heliocopter.

He was so happy when he learned that his wife was alive and safe, that he couldn't hold back the tears. He was reunited with her, and taken to the emergency room of the Lady of the Sea Hospital in Galliano, Louisiana.

Hale's eighteen-hour ordeal brought him to a fuller awareness of his own capabilities and limitations. When asked how much longer he could have lasted, he replied, "I don't know; but I do know one thing - no man is a match for an angry sea."

IN THIS ISSUE:

70 Pages in 7 Sections

THE HOUMA COURIER

Classified Ads On

Pages 8-9-10-11-A

In 92nd, Year -- No. 33   Houma, Louisiana 70360, Friday, August 15, 1969   Member The Associated Press   **TEN CENTS**

Houman Lives Thru Night of Wind, Rain

By Lenny LeBlanc

Sheer endurance, perseverance and knowledge of the sea through a series of trying events has probably saved the life of a Houma man who was found by a U. S. Coast Guard search helicopter from Grand Isle after spending a harrowing 17 hours afloat in the Gulf of Mexico, with nothing more to cling to than a seat cushion from his outboard.

Pushed by storm winds, high seas, and tides, James Hale, was picked up 20 miles offshore, almost 15 miles from a production platform off of Grand Isle where he and his wife, Helen, and a sister-in-law, Mrs. Nina Dupuy, were fishing from the previous day.

Exhausted, hungry, thirsty, and suffering from the beginning stages of exposure, Hale related a tale of desperation and frustration as he attempted to remain afloat during a night of storm-swept seas. His wife had spent a gruesome Sunday night and Monday morning with rescue personnel helping to search for her husband.

During the previous afternoon, heavy seas had caused a line securing their outboard boat to a production platform to break setting the outboard loose with Mrs. Hale in it. Hale, in attempting to swim out to the boat was swept away from the boat and platform by outgoing tides, while the boat was swept in another direction by increasing winds.

A Sunday Fishing Party

The Hales and Mrs. Hale's sister had left Grand Isle that

(Continued On Page Ten)

JAMES HALE and wife, Helen, are pictured above, with the outboard that almost cost him his life Sunday night. The only evidence of his 17-hour ordeal in the Gulf of Mexico waters was the cushion strap marks above his armpits. (Staff Photo)

I couldn't help but notice that these articles were written on the day after Hurricane Camille formed in the Gulf of Mexico.

Hurricane Camille was the second-most-intense tropical cyclone to strike the United States on record. Camille Quickly formed as a tropical depression on August 14th 1969 south of Cuba. The storm quickly intensified into a category 2 hurricane before striking the Western part of the Nation on August 15th 1969. While in the Gulf of Mexico, Camille rapidly intensified becoming a category 5 as it moved northward towards Louisiana.

Sunday morning to spend a day fishing. Seas were smooth and the weather showed no sign of approaching storms and inclement weather, as the party approached the platform located about ten miles offshore.

Towards midafternoon, seas became rough as the wind picked up. When it became evident that the weather would not improve but was becoming increasingly bad as the afternoon wore into evening, the fishing party decided to return to the island.

While in the process of returning fishing gear to the boat from the platform, the boat, with Mrs. Hale aboard, broke loose. Seas were already near six feet and the 14-foot outboard was immediately swept away from the platform. She attempted to start the outboard motor but was unsuccessful.

In the Water

Hale, realizing that seas were getting rougher and the boat was drifting fast, jumped in with a seat cushion and attempted to swim out to the boat.

Although a good swimmer, the tide and rough seas carried him south away from the platform while the boat, more vunerable to the effect of the wind, drifted

east.

In a whispery voice still hoarse from yelling at passing vessels during the night, Hale told Coast Guard officials after being rescued that while being swept away from the platform, he at first became frustrated at not being able to reach the boat, then thankful that he had, in a moment of thought, taken a flotation cushion with him.

In the meantime, Mrs. Dupuy, unable to leave the platform where she had been abandoned, watched her two fishing companions drift out of sight in separate directions, unable to do anything about either.

The accident happened at 7:00 Sunday evening, and Hale was still in the rough seas when it began to get dark. Knowing that help would not be forthcoming from his wife or sister-in-law, Hale said that he tried correcting his course of drift by swimming in order to approach several drilling platforms in the area.

After several exhausting attempts Hale finally settled down to just remaining afloat. He said that the only means of keeping his head out of the water was to place the cushion against his back and kick in a slow motion.

Thunderstorm

During the night an electrical thunderstorm came up threatening to make his plight of trying to remain afloat still worse. The sea, previously littered with seven and eight foot whitecaps, turned into thundering ten foot rollers with the tops of waves breaking over him.

The storm brought Hale five miles closer to shore and his spirits lifted as he spied a drilling platform and crew boat anchored nearby. Swimming again and yelling, he was swept within sixty feet of the boat, but no one aboard seemed to hear him. Several times during the night boats passed nearby but he was unable to signal them.

An interesting sidelight to his now desperate condition, was the abundance of phosphorus in the water after the storm. Hale said that by making a swirling motion in the water with his hands, thousands of tiny lights appeared all around him.

But not so interesting was the fact that the salt water was sapping the small amount of energy he had left, and the flesh on his hands and feet was becoming numb. Hale said that chills, which were only affecting the extremities of his limbs during the early hours of the

night, began to affect his whole body. The paddling motion to keep afloat slowed down and he had to force consciousness to accomplish easy motions.

Adrift

Meanwhile earlier during the night, Mrs. Hale, in the outboard, reached a like stage of desperation. She knew that the only way she could help her husband was to signal for help herself.

She attempted to start the boat motor several more times as darkness approached but the starting battery had run down during the repeated attempts. The battery did however provide enough current to operate a spotlight.

After dark she collected burnable material aboard the boat including towels and cardboard boxes, and soaked it all in gasoline. Throwing it overboard she tried to set it afire in order to attract attention, but the rough seas broke up the burning rubbish and snuffed out the flames in half of a minute.

Finally after signaling for several hours, a shrimp boat, the "Jeffrey Paul" out of Biloxi, pulled in close to investigate the signal. After taking her aboard, Mrs. Hale talked the shrimp boat captain into helping her look for her husband and sister.

On the way back to the production platform she had been set adrift from, the captain sent out a radio message to the U. S. Coast Guard at Grand Isle.

Mrs. Hale had been picked up at 10:30 p.m., and after hours of plowing through swelling seas, the shrimper reached the platform at 12:30 the following morning.

Mrs. Dupuy was pulled aboard after having to swim out from the platform. The shrimper could not approach because of high seas.

A coast guard cutter was dispatched immediately after the radio call was received from the shrimp boat but the cutter did not arrive upon the scene until three o'clock that morning. Both boats commenced a search pattern in the area.

Far Out to Sea

Little did they know, however, that Hale had been taken way out to sea by a second storm during the night, so that the pattern of search started way inshore from his position.

Later that morning another thunderstorm arose, this time out of the north. Fighting to keep on top of the water, Hale grew progressively weaker. Thirst became a real problem as he tilted his head up to catch rain water. During the night he picked up a dead fish floating in the water and put it inside his bathing suit, in case of hunger during the following hours.

The storm didn't last long, but had pushed him further out to sea and complicated the search pattern of the boats looking for him.

Morning Light and Hope

Morning light brought renewed hope for Mrs. Hale as a Coast Guard helicopter and two oil company helicopters joined the search.

Mrs. Hale, who, with her sister had been brought by this time to the Coast Guard station on Grand Isle, attempted to recruit further rescue help from private boat captains. There were few takers, she said, because the weather was still stormy offshore and seas were running over eight feet.

Two boats had been sunk Sunday night during rough seas, and survivors had been brought back to Grand Isle. Considering the circumstances, neither boat captains or the Coast Guard had much hope of finding her husband alive.

Alive

Very much alive, but barely kicking Hale, now twenty miles offshore, had a number of problems to contend with. He was rapidly drifting into a block area where there were few platforms, hence fewer crew boats. The weather kept most fishing boats inshore, and most of the other production platforms were nearly 100 miles out.

Morning light had brought the gaunt realization that the skin on his hands and feet had turned blue during the night from lack of circulation. The numb and tingling feeling had now spread all over his body.

Realizing also that he would have to eat something to maintain his feeble supply of energy, he tried to trap sea gulls in lieu of the dead and bloated fish he had been saving in his swimming trunks. He layed back in the water playing dead, but none of the gulls swooped down low enough for him successfully to reach.

Help!

While reaching out at one inquisitive bird, the slight gain of height brought a distant boat into his range of vision. The sky was hazy and seas were still breaking slightly, but successive inspections of the horizon brought the rigging of a shrimp boat into view. He realized then that the shrimper was headed in his direction, and had in all probability seen him.

Now waving and shouting, which was reduced to a hand in the air and a croak, Hale watched as the shrimper varied his course from one set to pull alongside him to one directly at him. The boat did not slow down as it reached his position.

In a panic, Hale kicked at the front hull of the boat, and managed to keep from getting caught underneath the keel. But too weak to push away, he was swept underneath the boat. Unhurt and apparently untouched by the propeller, he bobbed up out of the wash behind the shrimper. Hale waved again but the boat stayed on course and gradually drew out of range.

During most of the morning he had seen nothing resembling any kind of rescue vessel. Once a search helicopter had approached within several hundred yards, but after having apparently reached the end of its search pattern, it left the area.

He heard various noises seeming to approach and leave the area, but he couldn't be sure that he wasn't hearing things. Exposure and lack of sleep had reduced his range of perception to a bare minimum needed to survive.

The sun had not come out at all during the day, and Hale now thought that it was nearing dark, although it was just one o'clock Monday afternoon.

Rescue At Last

A droning sound suddenly closed in around him, and a surprised and thoroughly confused Hale turned around to confront a large red and white helicopter approaching. Looking like a bird from heaven, the copter tried to drop down towards him.

"I was waving like crazy this time," Hale said. "I didn't care if they were trying to put down next to me, I still wasn't sure they had actually seen me."

With the seas almost as rough as they were during the night, the Coast Guard helicopter could not put down a line. It circled the area awaiting the arrival of a Coast Guard cutter in the area. Five to ten minutes later the cutter pulled alongside and Hale motioned for a rope to be put down the side so that he could climb up.

"I had fantastic energy by that time," he said enthusiastically. The cutter stood away from him, instead, because heavy seas would have thrown him against the steel hull of the vessel. Two men jumped overboard with lines and helped him aboard.

Not realizing how drained of strength he was, he tried to walk on the deck and almost collapsed. The men aboard the cutter wrapped him in a blanket, strapped him into a basket and he was pulled up into the waiting helicopter, to be brought to a hospital in New Orleans.

When Hale was told that his wife was at the Coast Guard station in Grand Isle, he refused to go to New Orleans.

Since Hale appeared energetic enough to protest, the copter pilot set down on the heliopad at the station.

Reunion

His wife, who had been told of his miraculous rescue just moments before, awaited his arrival with the first visible signs of relief from her all night vigil.

Exhausted, hungry, thirsty, the weary Hale was finally united with his wife. After a few moments of thanks to the rescue crews, Hale quickly surrounded a big meal, now long overdue.

Wednesday morning, the recuperating Hale, at his residence in Houma, was able to talk. The only signs of his 17-hour ordeal being the exposed flesh around each arm where the straps of his flotation cushion had worn the skin away during the night.

"Being out there is the loneliest feeling in the world," he said.

"There is no one around, and you don't know if anyone is looking for you."

"Everything works on you," he said. You get tired as the energy is gradually drained from your body; the water removes the warmth from your body and a slow certain chill sets in, ebbing what little strength you have left."

In reply to a question concerning his henceforth wariness around salt water, he replied "No, it has given me more confidence."

"I now know what I can and cannot do," said the 28-year-old part time scuba diver and fisherman, who in real life around Houma, is an insurance representative for Metropolitan Life Insurance Company.

———O———

By all means I should have lost my life back then. So much was against me, so many incidents & threats occurred that would normally have struck me down. And I was pushed so, to the very end of my endurance. But yet lived – For What? Was I saved for some reason or purpose? I search constantly for this. I feel even today I have been living on borrowed time. Does this date and the coincidence of these events have some meaning? I will search for this.

Thurs 8/27/81
Up about 8:00 a.m., took a shortcut via a gravel road. It ended up being such a bad road we could hardly get through with the car. A short time later we got onto good highway. Then the left rear tire began coming apart. We drove to the nearest town (about 5 miles) and bought a new one. (Put this down for 8/24/81 – This is what I get for scribbling notes & writing in this book later). We got to Kalispell about 7:00 p.m. I went to the airport and checked the truck out – all was OK, just as I left it. We decided to leave it here as I would

need to have it here on Sat. to pick up
David & Alice at 11:30 p.m. We planned on
going into Canada & there would be no
need for Mom & Helen to drive me all the
way up the North Fork for my truck. It's
simpler to leave it here. Got to the camp
just after dark. Everything here was also
just as I left it on 8/10/81. Mom and Helen
looked around a little before we turned in &
went to sleep

Fri. 8/28/81
Mom and Helen looked around the place,
took pictures, etc. I changed the oil in
Mom's car, looked for Kevin's ring with
the metal detector, unpacked the car. As I
was taking the rocks out from under the tent
I found that one of them was Kevin's ring.
He had been sleeping on it all the time. He must have lost it the night we put
up the tent. We drove to the lake in Glacier Park and spent the afternoon
looking for rocks. I showed Mom and Helen the Polebridge store and went to
the Hostel for a shower.

Sat. 8/29/81
Mom and Helen left to go back home today. We drove through Glacier Park, shopped at Apgar, West Glacier and Columbia Falls. Helen bought a calculator she had been looking for. Drove to Kalispell to get brake pads for Mom's car. We changed them on the airport parking lot &

they left at 5:00 p.m. Then I went to Half Moon Supply & bought a picture window for the cabin, an old sewing machine, and a pair of ice skates. Then went back to work on washing cloths and got some groceries, back to the airport to call Pat & catch up on my writing. David and Alice flew in at 11:30 p.m. I drove to camp and went to bed about 2:00 a.m.

Sun. 8/30/81
Today it rained all day. Showed David & Alice around a little. We drove to Cyclone Mountain and walked up to the lookout tower (about 1 ½ to 2 miles). We spent a couple of hours talking to Nina (Alice's sister and Helen's brother's wife) and looking around. Couldn't see much with all the fog and rain. Shot a partridge on the way down, but couldn't find it. Somehow this night, the rain got between the tent and the visqueen under the tent and both David and I woke up in wet sleeping bags.

Mon. 8/31/81
Went to Polebridge to call chart house to check on Helen and Mom. They were to call in and leave word of their status. All was OK. We rigged the hoist for the logs, and worked on the cabin. We got 2 logs up today. The weather was nice all day. But began raining again just before midnight.

Tues. 9/1/81

We stayed in the tent until late morning as it was raining. I went to Polebridge to check my mail & to get water. Alice cooked breakfast. We couldn't work on the cabin in the rain – or at least didn't want to. It was also too rainy for sight-seeing, so we decided to go shopping around the little towns and to go look up an auction in Kalispell. Both David and I wanted some furs. We stayed in Columbia Falls this night.

Wed. 9/2/81

I had written a letter to Pat until early this morning. It is probably the last big letter I will write to her. I have little else to say - at least it seems it would do little good. Communication is poor now, and I plan to pull away soon. She is very distant and the sum of it all seems to add up to the end for our relationship. David & Alice were up and dressed before I heard them & woke up. It was 8:45 a.m. We went to the bank, to buy some mixing bowls that were on sale, to fill up with gas, and headed to Kalispell. Went to Wild Bill's

Outhouse near cabin, below Vance Hill

Trading Post and talked to Bill Brown, who is also my neighbor on the North Fork. We found out there were no auctions today. We went to a couple of garage sales. I decided to try to get a Montana hunting license (resident), but first needed to get a Montana driver's license. We went to the driver's license office and the clerk advised me to study the book first as the laws were different from Louisiana and she said several questions involved distance. I didn't have time to study the book and decided to try for the test anyway. I flunked it – I couldn't believe it. I had been driving since I was 12 years old & now I flunked the written exam. The laws were different though, and I had no way of knowing. It will be some time before I get over this – a blow to my ego, I guess. I got a book to study & will take the test again as soon as I get back to Kalispell. I need the license to get a resident hunting license. Also the bear season opens Saturday. We had the truck greased, ate, shopped a little and headed for the North Fork. The weather was fair & we put up one log before dark. David and Alice peeled a couple of logs also before dark.

Thurs. 9/3/81

Today was a beautiful day, the first pretty day since David and Alice got here. We worked all day on the log cabin - got 3 logs up today. We had all worked so hard, we went down to the Polebridge Hostel for a hot bath. We had been taking baths in the teepee using a large pan. Today the weather was cooler, as though fall is right around the corner.

Fri. 9/4/81

We woke up to a heavy fog – almost rain. I went down to the Polebridge store to call Helen, Mom and the Hursts. Mom and Helen got home Wed. night about 1:00 a.m. All went well and they had no trouble. As I was talking on the phone outside (in the wooden barrel) it began to snow a wet snow mixed with drizzling rain. The temperature was about 40°. The Hursts have been having difficulty with the help at the restaurant. Two key employees quit and the Mexican girl (Orilia) had a miscarriage and was home for a week. I went back to camp after getting my mail and finishing my letter to Pat. About time we finished eating, the weather began to clear. The rest of the day was beautiful.

We put up 3 more logs. Alice played with the chipmunks for a while until the Dziuk's dog came over and wanted to play with them also. The chipmunks didn't go along with that and disappeared. To backtrack – early this morning as I was driving out the driveway, I spotted a large moose in the Dziuk's meadow. I got David and Alice up and we got a glimpse of it just as it ran from behind a tree in the meadow into the woods on the far side.

Sat. 9/5/81

The weather was nice today – a cool crispness in the air as though fall is setting in. I worked on the cabin all day. Put up two and a half logs today. David and Alice went walking to the river below the camp for a few hours. When they returned,
they helped cut firewood and clean up the big pile of brush near the teepee. We all took a shower at the hostel about 10:00 p.m.

Sun. 9/6/81

I finished a log I began yesterday and put up another. David and I then went looking for firewood up Cyclone Mountain Rd. Alice stayed at camp and worked on Cleaning up the brush pile and stacking firewood. We were not

able to find any large enough trees that we could get to with the truck. We ran across a covey of grouse and shot 2 of them with the .22 rifle. We also saw a couple of deer on the way back. We got back just before dark and went to the Northern Lights Saloon to eat.

Mon. 9/7/81

David, Alice and I drove down to Spruce Creek Rd. and found some large dead standing trees that we could get near with the truck. We cut enough firewood to load the truck and I went to camp. I stayed and worked on the cabin. Alice also stayed and worked on burning the brush and stacking firewood. Paula Dziuk helped her for a while. David and Chuck Dziuk went back to Spruce Creek for more firewood. He returned about dark with another load. He had cut another load and had stacked it near the road. I went with him to get it. We changed the oil in the truck and went down to Spring Creek to rinse out the back bed. We took showers at the Hostel and got to bed about 2:00 a.m.

Tues. 9/8/81

We cooked the two grouse with some potatoes for breakfast, went to Polebridge for the mail (left the 9mm pistol and the chain saw at the Dziuk's). We drove over the "Going to the Sun Rd." in Glacier Park to the town of St. Mary, where we washed our cloths. We then crossed the Canadian border via Highway 17 and drove through Waterton Lakes to the town of Pincher Creek. We ate and spent the night here. The rate of exchange on Canadian money is about $1.20 to $1.00, but the local merchants exchange for only $1.10 to $1.00. We are getting "ripped off," so we will go to the bank tomorrow to get the correct exchange rate.

Wed. 9/9/81

We went to the bank this morning to exchange our money. We ate at a little café in Pincher Creek and drove on to Banff, Alberta. Ca. We bought another "monkey puppet" for Kevin and spent the afternoon going through the shops. We went to the Banff Springs Hotel and looked around the place for some time. The place impressed us. It looked like an elegant old castle. We went to the lounge and had a drink (for an hour or two). It was late; but we couldn't find a hotel in Banff that had a vacancy, and drove on to Lake Louise. We also couldn't find a place to stay there. We ended up in a hostel sleeping in bunk beds with a bunch of other guys and girls, and had no covers. It was cold. David and Alice covered themselves with a sleeping bag that was not being used by anyone on a vacant bunk. I covered with my down coat, but ether my feet were cold or my shoulders were. The coat would not cover all of me. I alternated between my feet and my shoulders all night. About 3:00 a.m. the owner of the sleeping bag came in (a fellow from Switzerland) and looked in everyone's bunk for his bag. But when he learned that they had no covers, he went in his car and got another bag for himself. He seemed nice about the whole thing – also seemed drunk. P.S. We also visited Bow Falls, and Hot springs near Banff. We took pictures of the hotel just after dark from Bow Falls.

Thurs. 9/10/81

We ate a huge breakfast at Lake Louise Post Hotel. We spent all day walking the mountain trails around Lake Louise. Saw three avalanches as they fell from the glacier high above Lake Louise. They produced a roaring thunder that was very impressive as the snow and ice fell a couple of thousand feet off a cliff. One avalanche began just as we were looking at the end of the glacier; it was huge. We could see the huge end of the glacier break off before we heard the thunder. It seemed to all

move in slow motion. As it hit the lower cliffs and the ground below, a huge white cloud slid across the ground for perhaps a thousand feet, and hit the cliff wall of the mountain on the opposite side of the valley. The cloud just climbed up the wall in slow motion, and rose high into the air before falling to the earth - a spectacular sight that seemed to shake the ground as it

thundered nearly a mile from our observation point. We visited two tea

houses, walked to Agnes Lake and Minor Lake before returning to the Lake Louise Lodge just before dark. We had walked about 10 miles up and down mountains all day, and were thankful for the big breakfast this morning. We drove on to the Columbia ice fields this night. Saw a deer and three mountain goats. We found out that there were no other places to stay within 30 miles of the ice fields except for the hotel just across the road. They had only 1 room left. It was a "rip off" at $43.00. No food, no bath tub, no heat, 3 single beds etc. etc. But we had no other choice and stayed here for the night. We ordered a ham sandwich and a glass of milk each – cost plus we lost $2.00 in the exchange rate. We ran out of Canadian money. The wind outside was cold and blew perhaps 20 mph in gusts. It came right off the ice fields and blew right through the cracks in the windows. It blew the curtains as though the window was open. We slept with extra covers.

Fri.9/11/81
Got up and had a roll for breakfast. Prices were outrageous so we decided to eat down the road. We went to see the ice fields. We rode a snowmobile that was a greyhound bus that was converted by putting caterpillar tracks under it.

We drove on to the North Fork (camp) and got there about 11:00 p.m. everything between the ice fields and the border was a "rip off." Gas was as high as $1.85 per gallon (American). We stopped to eat in Columbia Falls.

Also spent more time photographing mountain sheep near Radium Hot Springs. Alice had a sore throat for the last few days and today wasn't feeling too good. I hope she doesn't get sick.

Sat 9/12/81
Up at 4:30a.m. And to the airport in Kalispell. David and Alice left for Dallas on Frontier airlines at 7:05a.m. I was sad to see them go. They are two of my favorite people and proud to have them as my brother and sister-in-law. I called Pat from the airport. She seemed happy and adjusted to Pennsylvania. I could read something was not right though - perhaps her attitude was a cover up? – I didn't have much to say to her – just listened. I was so sleepy I slept in the truck in the parking lot for a couple of hours. I bought some supplies, food, washed my clothes, and wrote letters and post cards. Mailed letters and Kevin's puppet monkey I bought for him in Banff, Canada.
Went by to see Bill Brown's new log cabin. They weren't home. Went to a campground and took a shower. Called PWP (Parents Without Partners) and went to visit at a member's home. They invited me to a dance at the Eagle Hall. They were all much older than I, but I stayed until 12:30a.m. I got to North Fork about 2 a.m.

Sun 9/13/81

I slept late this morning, went to Polebridge store for mail. Put up 2 logs on the cabin and started peeling another after dark and got my 9mm pistol and chain saw from Dziuk's and visited the Costellos for a while. I have thought about Dad quite a bit the last couple of weeks. He struggled most of his life, had hard times with Richard (my brother), business, etc. and didn't seem to get much pleasure out of life. He didn't do the things he wanted to. Wish he could have come here. He never got to see the big mountain country, smell the fresh air, drink water from the cool spring, etc. I was planning for him and Mom to come up here when I got things set up. I must learn from this, perhaps

make his life a little more meaningful. I do live my life for the time with reasonable plans for the future. Received a very mild signal today – perhaps nothing – but I'm staying in tune with myself. There are signs that I may have

a serious fight for my life sometime in the near future. The time element is vague, but definitely within a year. I must keep alert. I do not have the love, will, etc. that I need for the drive for life if stamina is required of me.

Mon. 9/14/81

Up rather early today but didn't feel like working on the cabin. I may regret it if winter sets in early, But I spent most of the day grading the driveway, cutting firewood, and straightening up around camp. Later this afternoon I worked on the cabin and nearly finished fitting one log. I am completely alone now, no one to talk to or to depend upon if I need help. I seem to be tuning in to the feel of the air and the things around me. The wind is different now, a steady crisp breeze from the N.W. I feel that fall is very near. Heard the bugle of the bull elk across the valley for the first time today.

The North Fork Road

Tues. 9/15/81

I went to Polebridge for my mail. First time since I've been here that I haven't gotten any mail. I called Helen to relay me via her Watts line to several people I needed to contact about Dad's business as well as mine. Tried to call Mom, but no answer. I was to come back to the store later this afternoon and call again. When I returned someone was on the phone and I couldn't reach Helen. I will try tomorrow. I worked on the cabin all day. Had trouble with one log, it was crooked. I put ¾ steel pegs in it and pulled it straight with the block and tackle. I drove the pegs in holes I had drilled so it would stay straight. This took most of the afternoon. I put up another log across the top of

the back window. Started on another log in front just as it was getting dark. I ate a big supper, took a bath, and wrote several postcards. The Dziuks' came by today. Think I will take a couple of hours off and join them. Also ran into Tom Riemer at the store. He and another friend are going to try to bugle in some elk and want me to take some pictures (in a week or two). The moon has been full and exceptionally bright the last few nights.

Wed. 9/16/81

Paula Dziuk was sick today – we didn't go pick berries. I went to the Polebridge store to call Mom and several other people on business. Put up one log on the front of the cabin. Began peeling another one for the side and realized it was rotten. Pulled in another, it was rotten in spots also. I have only one log left for this side and it is crooked. Hope the Dziuks' get their logs hauled in soon. They will have some extra that I can use. Went to Spruce Creek and cut a truck load of firewood. Chuck Dziuk came with me. I got back after dark and split a truck load of firewood by lantern light. The moon came up full and bright just about time I was quitting. Night before last I kept hearing all night, distant sounds as though someone was playing short bursts of notes on some type of pipe instrument. Last night I began hearing it more frequently. I got up and sat on the edge of the bluff. The sounds were coming from across the river in Glacier Park. They were elk bugling and only the high

notes were reaching me. They were really active all night – one every 5 minutes or so. It's about midnight now, and I haven't heard any yet. I wonder why? The weather is the same as last night. Also I haven't seen our friendly deer around camp in several weeks. Just beginning to realize that it is probably because hunting season is near. They seem to know, and head for parts unknown. Felt lazy today, had to push myself to work.

Thurs. 9/17/81
Went to pick huckleberries with the Dziuk's today for a couple of hours. I got about 1 gallon. Will try to make jam with them. Had a sandwich at their house. Their dog "Rascle" got into it with a skunk under the Northern Lights Saloon at Polebridge. He is now known as "skunk dog" And the smell in the Saloon is intolerable. Paula, Chuck and I went back to Spruce Creek to cut more firewood. We brought in another load. I pulled a 25' log and set it up on the wall – didn't notch it. I am beginning to feel bad. Hope I didn't catch Paula's flu (virus). I've been around her and her family all day. Also I drank water out of the same carton she did today

Fri 9/18/81

Something kept making noise around the tent last night. I shined the spotlight out a couple of times, but didn't see anything. I work up this morning feeling like I had been run over by a logging truck. I have a full fledged case of the flue – headache, sore throat, back of eyes hurt, hurt all over. Went to Polebridge store to get mail and to call Mrs. Hurst. Came back to camp and decided to try and sweat it out. Worked in the cabin all day. Ate aspirin and drank maybe 2 gallons of fluid. Really felt bad today – very weak. Fitted one log, pealed another. And just about fitted it before dark. Went to bed with chills and fever.

Saturday 9/19/81

Stayed in the tent until late morning. It is a miserable, rainy day outside. The flu still has its grip on me today. But at least I don't feel as bad as yesterday. Didn't get to sleep until 3 a.m. Worked on fitting a log between rains. And studied for my driver's test during the rain. Finished fitting one log & set another on top of wall – at least I did something today.

Sun 9/20/81

Its 4:30 a.m. – I can't sleep – Fever and chills kept me awake earlier, but now I'm feeling better. Mostly have been thinking about Pat. Wish I could turn off the thinking machine – I am so in need of sleep. I have been forced lately to look at the other side of Pat – something I didn't want to do, but really should. She has been so cold and distant since I left Lafayette (actually when she got to Pa., about 2 weeks later). I remember how cold she was last summer when I went up to Pa. to drive her and her kids back home to La. Never felt such coldness from anyone before. Didn't think I deserved this. She had asked me to come up, and when I did I felt so unwanted there by her. The trip home was torture with her kids fighting etc. her coldness etc. and me obligated to take them home. I had no control of the situation – except pressure. I spent $700.00 to get them home, and it goes on record as the worst trip I have ever made. Will never forget it. Many other times I noticed a coldness or lack of warmth but thought it was just my sensitivity. In looking back on this in a different light, I see something I do not want regardless of the reason. Have been considering marriage to Pat. There is too much coldness from the rest of the world to have it from someone so near. Must have a warm place in my life to counteract it. It seems my mind is beginning to turn from Pat. Reconsidering so many things also – I thought she was such a good girl. Guess she still is in many other ways – she will always be special to me for her good qualities. It is so mentally and physically exhausting to reverse the mind's chemistry for someone so near. (At least for me it is) Woke up at 10:00 a.m. – It's a beautiful day outside. Also, I think

> Love is a free feeling that cannot be chained. It cannot be directed, but indeed is itself the director.
>
> James Hale

Old Homestead 1/4 mile South of Polebridge Meadow

I've got the flu whipped. Feel much better today, only a mild sore throat. Worked on putting up a log over the back window, the small logs between the door and the picture window, didn't quite get to boring the holes and driving the rods in before dark. The air turned chilly much faster tonight. I noticed this happens on clear nights, and tonight the sky is crystal clear.

Mon. 9/21/81

Today was another miserable rainy day – just the opposite from yesterday. It snowed heavily and constantly in the mountains all day today. It snowed down about 500' above my elevation. It rained here all day – only an occasional snowflake. This is the first good snowstorm of the winter. I'm curious to see what the mountains look like when the storm clears. The logs were too slippery to climb on and the log over the front window is not tied down with rods yet. I decided not to chance working up there today. Not much more I can do up there anyway until more logs come. I worked on clearing the brush pile behind the cabin, and stacking firewood there. Split some firewood also. Wrote and read some during heavy rain. I'm concerned about getting a hard snow here before I can get a roof on the cabin. Temperature was near 35° shortly after dark. I was wet and cold through and through. Hadn't eaten today and was hungry. Decided to go to the saloon to get a bowl of hot soup, and to the Hostel to soak in a hot bathtub. When I returned to camp the sky was crystal clear. It still amazes me how near the stars look up here, how many there are, and how they twinkle with such a sharp, clear looking light. It touches me inside, makes me feel good – it is though I am closer to the god I believe in. The pollution and city lights hide such beauty from us. The clouds have not cleared the mountains yet, but there seems to be more light coming from the north than any other part of the sky. There may be a display of northern lights tonight.

Tues. 9/22/81

Up at 1:30 a.m. – no northern lights – back in the sack. Up again at 9:00 a.m. – the weather is dreary and rainy. More snow in the mountains. Went to Polebridge store to make more business phone calls. Spent maybe 3 hours there. As I was talking on the phone it began to turn cold with a good steady east wind. Got my mail and returned to camp. Later today the rain stopped and I was able to work on putting the rods in along the window (front) and a small corner log next to the door

Hey Dad!   9/16

    And you said it upset me not to get any mail!
Sorry I didn't write sooner but I've got problems
and I was just letting them compound interest till
I could get your advice. Bear's had a hard life
since we got back, he says he doesn't like school,
too many people petin ya! (I like school thought and
trying for all "A's, and doing it so far.) The first
day of school me & Bear would walk down the halls
of crowded people, I never heard silence like that
before, and every once in a while a scream. One
teacher had me going to the office till she found
out it's a muppet. And at the games I went out
on the side of the field with the cheerleaders
and turned around toward the stands, Atlelato!
3/4s of the people's eyes were on Bear.

    Ima do great in school this year. 1st
hour I have Biology (the one I failed), I have
my favorite teacher in the school and so far out
of about 3 or 4 hundred pts I'm 2 pts off.
2nd hour is Art, Miss Robinson had something
to do with putting the people she wanted in
that class, cause I'ls all the same people I had
last year (all the top Artists), the and a friend
asked to have a special Art (Advanced drawing)
instead of painting; and my picture's entered in
the Art show, so I don't have to tell you what kind
of grades I'm making. 3rd hour is composition
the whole class is kinda rusty at writing but I
should turn out an A. Last hour is free Enterprise,
we call the teacher Miss WAC short for the WAMs
or the B____, she's really some kinda teacher.

This is her second year in teaching and she's trying for a reputation in mean, rough, toughness, but all she's being is difficult. Anyway, we took her test yesterday and when we got in class today this was written on the board!

	1 - A
95-100 A	3 - B's
88-94 B	11 - C's
79-87 C	1 - D'
70-78 D	15 - F's

I though sure I was that 1-D but it turned out to be the second highest in class, one of the B's, I got a 94, 1 point from an A. The guy who got the A had a cheat sheet and without it couldn't find his big toe.

Lisa's causing a lot of trouble, she's been skipping school because she rides to school with some friends. Leo + mom went away for the weekend so she was to stay here, but she shucked + jived her way into staying with her friends. It's the hardest thing to tell grandma it's not her fault. I have this Jim Beam 2 gallon whisky bottle that I save coins in, when I left <s>it had</s> for the summer a good 5 inches of a good mixture, when I came back it shrank a couple of inches, two weeks went by and I went to pick it up and there's a half an inch of pennies. So mom says "what do you want me to do!" she kinda right but going to buy damn ass stuff with a bunch of guy's at dark + smoking at grandma being called to the office every other day... she's B's house. my sister something has to be done.

All mom says is I don't want to argue with her.   huh!

Last but not least — Kevin Hale. As one Boss said to another " about an Accountant he wanted to fire "I'm having trouble in the Financial Department". See I'm trying to start me a businessin grandpa's shop called Custom Unlimited. An Audio shop says people come in all the time wanting stereo cabinets so I have a good demand there from what I hear. I also can make any thing the people want out of wood... A lady wants me to build her a Gazebo. I going tomorow to tell her it'll cost near a thousand, a good 400's hundred profit if she wants it. I got kind of a part time job today at custom vans in Lafayette. The guy seems to like me & what I say about my airbrush & customizing but I'm still a phone number on the wall. I decided the best way to get him intrested is to prove it to him, so I thoug a little shag carpet & a touch of wood could really fixup the inside of truck & then buy a couple of bottles of paint for my air brush and add a touch of class to the outside. And go show it to him cause I seen the guy work who works there now and with a little practice could be much better than him. So I go tell moma that I can work for mr, bob this weekend & get a few dollars, can I buy a few things so I can get started. WHAT! ARE YOU CRAZY! . See thr bob has trouble with something about taxes & doesn't want to hire me; I wont go work in fast food joint, I want to learn my trade, After all this is my last year in school and I don't want to be a burger pusher. So when I get

a little bit of gold momma takes it because I
owe money for gas, insurance + the silver
shoe laces for her boots, so I cant buy the
slightest little thing to get my business off the
ground + just think of when I does land it
will no matter how I get the money, all the
gold I'll be rolling in for kids at school wanting,
right now, a wood dash board, the stereo
place wanting stands. All it would take
would be a couple of weeks savings + I could
print some cards, put ads in papers, I really
~~think~~ know I could work my ass off and
make money for my VAN.

time for home work
better git going.   let me know whats
                         happening up there with
                         the cabin + such.

                   your FAVORITE son

        I love you dad. Kevin

Wed. 9/23/81

The weather is much better today. Partly cloudy and 40°. Went to Polebridge to make calls to people I missed yesterday. Peeled 5 logs for the gable ends. Went to tom Latenburg's to talk to him about getting some more logs to me and asking permission to cut firewood on his place. He couldn't get in touch with the trucker who hauled for him, but said he would try to have some on his flatbed trailer for me tomorrow. I cut a truckload of firewood and went to camp. Visited with the Costello's this evening and ate a bowl of stew with them. Came back about 11:00 p.m. and took a bath. The temperature was 26° – colder than usual at this hour, and especially cold for an outside bath in a pan of water.

Thurs 9/24/81

A cold 20° this morning. Went to Polebridge store to call Mom – finally got to her. Had several things to talk about (mostly Dad's business). Went to Tom Ladenburg's to push for some more logs. John Dziuk said his logs would be hauled next Thursday. That was another delay and I have had too many. I told him Tom said he would bring me some on his flatbed truck and I would prefer not to wait till Thurs. Went to cut more firewood. About time I got a truckload cut, here came John Dziuk with the flatbed loaded with logs. Went to camp, helped him pull the logs off with my truck, unloaded my firewood, and went back for another load of firewood. Got back just before dark, unloaded the firewood and decided to take my bath before it got too cold. Paula and Chuck came over and wanted me to come to their house to have birthday cake. It was their Mom's birthday, and some friends were there. Came back about 10: 00 p.m., ate, took a bath, and wrote to Mac and Kevin.

View of West Glacier National Park from the cabin

Fri. 9/25/81

Up 5:00 a.m., Went to Tom Riemer's to get him up. We were to go to Sullivan's Meadow in Glacier Park to "bugle in" some elk. A girl named Rosalind came by about 7:00 a.m. to take pictures also. Got back to Polebridge about noon. Didn't see or hear any elk. Saw several deer and some fresh bear droppings. It began to rain. I got my mail and went to camp. Worked between rain showers to peel a log and put it on top of cabin. Pulled another in but rain kept me from work. Just before dark the temperature was 38° – will be cold and wet tonight. Went to the Hostel for a bath and Saloon to ask John Frederick if I could use his log roller again. Had a beer and went to get the log roller at Tom Riemer's house. Today it snowed at camp for 10 or 15 minutes.

Sat. 9/26/81

Weather chilly in morning but warmed up to maybe 45° or 50° by 2:00 p.m. Peeled a log and put it on top of the cabin. Fitted another and worked on door opening. John Dziuk came by today. We had a beer and talked for a couple of hours. Didn't get as much done as I would have liked to today. It gets dark so early now – somewhere between 8:00 p.m. and 8:30 p.m.

Sun 9/27/81

Today was a rather uncomfortable day. Woke up to 34° and snow on the ground. Sat in the truck until I heard a weather forecast. 80 percent rain today and 60 percent tomorrow. It was raining a drizzling rain. I needed food and to wash clothes in town, and was to pick a day like today to do it. But today is Sunday and needed to go to the bank. Decided I couldn't afford to waste 2 days so I got out in the mess and went to work. Peeled 4 logs until dark. Didn't want to work up on the wall – too slippery. By dark I was tired, wet and cold. Went to saloon to eat and Hostel to sit in hot bathtub – thanks for the Hostel on days like this.

Mon 9/28/81

The rain seemed to quit sometime before daylight, but it drizzled on and off all morning. Temperature hanging in at about 40°, not as bad as yesterday. Pulled in a 35 foot log and peeled it. Put the first floor joist up on the 2nd floor. Really difficult getting this log in place. Worked on peeling another log before dark – didn't finish. Today I slipped and fell through the floor joist –

135

only skimmed shin and bruised ribs. Must be more careful when logs are wet. Today I am sore from pushing so much in the cold weather. Arms and back hurt – even my ribs. Must be losing more weight. It even hurts to sit down. I need more padding when peeling logs.

Tues 9/29/81
Overcast this morning, but looks like it may clear. I am out of Coleman fuel, cash, low on food etc. Decided to take today to go into town for business and supplies. Picked up mail at Polebridge and gave 2 guys (Hans Peter from Germany and David? from Seattle) a ride into Kalispell. Met them last night at the Hostel. Took driver's test and missed one question (the correct answer wasn't in the multiple choice so they didn't take off for my guess). Went to get my hunting and fishing license (finally). Five licenses in all, I think. Went to court house and got copies of the land deeds which Buster Schreiler never sent to me. Arranged to license my snowmobile. Went to Bill Brown's store to deliver message from Costello. Picked up Costello's spare tire for him. Washed clothes, bought supplies, bought food, transferred my truck insurance

to Montana via Time Insurance agency. Called Mom and she said Derouen's Lot Leveling took the $600 check she sent them, and which they agreed with me to settle for, and his attorney sent her a letter stating that we still owe more money. This is an underhanded move on Derouen's part, and I asked Mom to try to stop payment on the check. Will decide how to handle this when she finds out if the check can be stopped. Went to an auction and bought a pair of downhill ski boots for $4.00 and a

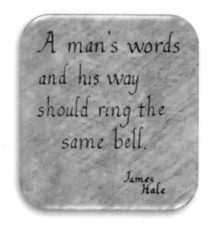

Styrofoam ice bucket full of pencils for $5.00. Ate at the Night Owl in Columbia Falls and to camp 2:00 a.m. Couldn't get to sleep until just after daylight – too much on my mind. Sally Costello drove into camp for her spare tire at 10:00 a.m. I got up and gave it to her, but I was so sleepy. I went back to bed. Slept a couple more hours and went to order food at a "food ordering" pantry near Polebridge. Back to camp around 4:00 p.m. Peeled 2 logs. The weather is getting better now – Perhaps tomorrow I can get something done. It feels like the last 2 days were wasted.

Thurs. 10/1/81

A pretty day today – Sunny and high around 60°, first pretty day in a long time. Peeled a log this morning, but the big muscle under my left shoulder blade really complained. It was painful to finish the log. Don't think I pulled it, just overworked. Will have to slack off using it too much until it can "catch up". I noticed the other side is sore too. Fitted the log over the front door, and drove in one rod before dark. Cut the opening for the picture window after dark and put another log up for the loft floor joist. John Dziuk came by for a few minutes before dark. Think he must have wanted something, perhaps some help at his house, but he never said. Gave him 100 pencils for his kids.

Fri. 10/2/81

Awakened by John Dziuk. He wanted to talk to me about the construction of my roof. The day was clear and rainy. Went to Polebridge to get mail and call Mom. People on the phone for nearly 2 hours before I could get through. Back to camp to eat around noon. The weather began to clear. Peeled 3 logs and set them atop the cabin. Talked to Kevin this morning and have been disturbed all day. He is unhappy. Also got a depressing letter from him today.

He is developing attitudes that are and will continue to bring him pain and unhappiness. No one, including myself, has been able to get through to help him. I must concentrate my thoughts to this problem. Today I thought about my Dad, as I have often times since I've been back. I get so week I must quit what I'm doing and sit down. I then begin to cry for a spell. Can't pinpoint any single reason for this – just so many thoughts.

Hey DAD

    than that's a nice car, talk about a couple of years straight of work on that thing, I bet it's been in a car show or two

    Nothin much good to talk about here, every things kinda going down hill for me! Mom, Leo, Grandma Bernice pushing - pushing - pushing for me to go work at Burger King or something. They might be pushing too far dad, I'm really a basket case, I keep telling them I wouldn't couldn't won't go work at a job like that! A big business things like that, no one cares who you are just flip the burgers, bag the groceries, And you know that I can't take working under some one, but if I could just go to a place small and that I would really do something like at a body or upholstery shop. What I really want is to get my business started, customizing interiors of cars, get me some cards printed up, ads in the paper... people want that. I know I've head enough at school, I just don't have the money. I'm so mixed up I really don't know what I want or what to do or where to go. Ahale's the only person that could understand me, but Grandma doesn't really know about what I'm trying to do or how much I can do. Each time I hear I can't use you I really gets to me, know one knows how bad I want to work, but my kinda work By the time you get this letter I will have turned Lafayette upside down.

    — no experience
    no job

Sat 10/3/81
Awakened by Jerry Costello. He was bringing my hand saw back. He had gone to Columbia Falls yesterday and I asked him to have someone set it for me. I had it sharpened Tues. But the man did not set it. It would bind so bad I couldn't use it. He was unsuccessful in finding anyone who could set it. The

tenderness in my right arm is coming back. Have felt it for about a week, but today it is really hurting. I began taking aspirins for it today. Hope it holds off from getting worse – This could stop me completely. Tried to use my left arm as much as possible, but must swing the axe with my right arm. Peeled and put up another log for the floor joist. Roughed in 9 of the 10 notches for the floor joist. It began to snow just about dark. Weather today was cold and overcast, but I'm thankful it didn't rain. 30° before 8:00 p.m. Will have a cold night tonight.

Sun 10/4/81
Today was a pretty sunshiny day. Temperature got up to 40°, fitted the ten notches for the floor joist (left) and fitted a log over the back window. Set another 25 foot log on top of cabin. This and the next log will be slow – 7 notches in each log. Today I feel like I reached a major

stage of the cabin (finishing the second floor). 12 more logs and I will be at the roof level – will take about a week to get there. Snow for 10 or 15 minutes today. Temperature at 8:00 p.m. – 26°. Taking a bath in this temperature is getting old fast. The water changes to vapor so fast it looks like my whole body is on fire – strange. But inside I am freezing. My toes sting when I put them in the pan of lukewarm water.

Mon 10/5/81
Went to Polebridge at 8:30 a.m. to call Mrs. Hurst. Missed her Fri. and need to talk about pictures and finance. Someone was on the phone again for nearly an hour and I missed her again. Talked to Helen and my Mom. It seems the truck quit on Kevin and he left it on the side of the road. Someone came along and stole it. Was a cold 20° and very foggy. I talked to Bettie at the store and played with a cube puzzle until the fog lifted. Fitted the long log over the floor joist today.

Tues 10/6/81

Went to Polebridge to call Mrs. Hurst and get mail. Finally got to her. She said Kevin had taken Helen's car and ran away. I called Helen – she thinks he is headed for David's in Dallas. I think so too. Kevin is really having problems now. I have spent 10 hours trying to compose a letter to him, but I'm not half through it yet. Went to Dziuk's to ask if I could use their oven to bake a cake for a "potluck" dinner tonight at the saloon. Worked 3 or 4 hours on the cabin today. Quit around 5:00 p.m. to go to the "potluck" dinner. There were 60 or so people there. And the food was excellent – best meal I've had since I've been here.

Wed. 10/7/81

Raining this morning. Decided to peel logs rather than climb on top of the wall. Called Helen at 12:00 noon. Kevin was at David's house in Dallas. He was sorry for what he did. But I didn't talk to him. I will finish my letter to him and mail it Friday. He will go back home with David and Alice this weekend. They had planned to visit Mom this weekend anyway. I peeled 2 logs and the rain cleared. Notched five of the 7 notches on the log over the left before dark. I began peeling a third log by lantern light, and the big muscle on my left back began cramping again. I couldn't pull the draw knife too hard with my right arm because of the tenderness, so I had to quit. Hope my body will hold up until I finish the roof – then I can slack off a little. Went to Hostel to soak in the bathtub.

Thurs. 10/8/81

Just after daylight this morning a deer came running into camp stomping his feet, and making a lot of noise. He stopped just in front of the tent door, and was quiet for a minute. I just lay still. He then walked out of camp, and across the driveway stomping his feet as he went. He didn't know where I was and was trying to get me to move. He didn't snort and his actions indicated a buck – a good sized fellow. It was raining again – haven't seen good weather in a while now. Finished cutting the last 2 notches on the log over the left and fitted the log and notches. This took quite a while as there are 7 notches on this log. Bored holes and drove 12 pins in the loft joists and 2 for securing the logs on each side of the stovepipe hole. Pulled in another log and began peeling it just before dark. Finished it by lantern light, but the tenderness and the muscle cramping in my back are really bothering me. Found a bottle of ascription and some vitamins. Started taking them tonight.

FROG FESTIVAL
RAYNE, LOUISIANA

Fri 10/9/81
Went to get my mail this morning. Went to the Hostel to bring John Frederick a frog poster, and to sit at the table there to copy a letter I wrote to Kevin. He wouldn't be able to read it as it was. I hadn't finished by 2:00 p.m. and the postman leaves at 2:30 p.m. I had a letter to Mac and I couldn't finish the one to Kevin in time. Mailed letter to Mac. Called about my income tax, gave Karen Feather 10 posters to sell on consignment at the Polebridge store and went back to camp. Fitted log across back of cabin and peeled another by dark.

Sat. 10/10/81
Pretty day today – sunshine and high of 45°, finished peeling 2 logs I started and had to stop because of tenderness. Fitted 2 logs and put another atop the cabin. Finished letter to Kevin and gave it Dziuks to mail tomorrow rather than waiting until Tues. Don't know if it will help him, but it's all I can do for now.

Letter to Kevin

Kevin,

Your last letter & phone conversation were very upsetting to me. I know you are struggling to find your way in life and to organize your thoughts as to who you want to be. You feel you know enough to be independent, and are developing a mind of your own. This is a natural thing, and necessary for you to be able to stand on your own two feet. I didn't seem to have the problems that many kids your age have. But I want you to know that I did go through the same thing, thought the same thoughts, felt the same things etc. Because of this I may be of some help to you if you are willing to listen and to think about what I have to say.

The problem is though, I don't know if you are listening to me or anyone. Perhaps you feel as strongly about yourself that you are only listening to Kevin. If you block out the world and take in nothing that anyone tells you, and interpret things only the way you want to, then I see you cheating yourself out of a limitless amount of experience and learning that others have had & can clue you in on. A wise man would tap this resource to the maximum so he can live his life and direct his limited experience (you can do only so much in one life) in a way that would make him the happiest. You don't have to "experience" everything to know what it's all about – nor do you have time to experience everything. But man is given a high ability to "reason" things out. He can "associate" things people say to him with experiences he has had himself, and can "imagine" how they would be. This is learning from others.

I am one person who cares about you and can be straightforward with you. My greater gain would be to see you happy. I have nearly 40 years of very

146

active & diversified experiences in my life, and as I've said before, I feel I have lived the lives of several old men (I have never had an idle day in my life). In addition to this I, more than any person I know, have studied people. I know a great deal of what makes the human machine tick, what affects people, how they will react, and where they will end up. Much of these answers I have found within myself.

Now if you are wise enough to tap this resource, then I am willing to tell you what I have learned. First of all people are going to give you all kinds of advice. When they do, they are telling you the conclusions they have drawn based on experiences they have had in their own life. Since everyone's lives are as different as their fingerprint, most advice will probably not exactly "fit" your life. But you still should listen to it. And try to figure out where they are coming from. Perhaps you can use a little piece here and a little piece there to "fit" your life. Everyone has a story and a reason, and I've said before, "A wise man can learn even from a fool." It is an art in itself to learn what advice to take and what to throw away, a lot of reasoning and a lot of years of practice to become confident.

I have found though that if many people are giving me the same advice, or saying the same thing to me, and it is not what I believe, then I must go back to scrutinize & reexamine where my belief came from. It is rare that everyone is wrong and I am the only one right. A person should always remain flexible to change his beliefs if it is "reasonable" to do so. Often times you lose your belief on only a fact or two, or on limited experience because that's all you have. But as you gain new facts or experience that shed a new and different light on the subject, and you can see the whole picture differently, then you should change your belief. It takes a strong man to admit (especially to himself) that he was wrong. At this stage in your life you must realize that you are losing most of your beliefs on fewer facts & experiences than most people who are older than you and have more facts & experiences behind them. To remain firm in spite of the facts they present to you could cause you great unhappiness. Keep ideals high but reasonable and in reach – don't just say I'll have a lot of money – it takes much to do this or everyone would be rich. You can look at it like your brain is a computer that has been fed information for 17 years now. It now has enough information to begin operation on its own. But your computer has not yet had enough practice or experience to be highly efficient, nor can it do advanced calculations in competition with other computers that have a great deal more information to work with. If you always look at yourself in this manner all through your life, then you can better put yourself in perspective as to who you are. It will help you to be reasonable with yourself. So you don't take too big a bite of something just because your appetite (emotions, ego) drive you to do so.

Now the reason I am saying this is because I have observed you as an outsider. I see that you are taking bites too big to handle. And you are making yourself unhappy because you can't get what you want. You are not listening to reason but are trying to convince yourself & others that it doesn't apply to you. You are listening more to your emotions than to reason. (More on this later). There are many steps you must take one at a time. And many things you must learn before you get the grand prize. Look at it this way – If it didn't take much experience, reasoning, hard work & suffering, everyone would be millionaires. It is the person who is willing to reason well, gain experience, work hard and suffer for it that gets the rewards. If you look around you, you can see there are not many people willing to do this – but this is what it takes. Look at me here – after 3 months I am still grinding my way to a log cabin. I work in 28° weather & raining (Not the pretty weather you and I had). Most people would have quit long before now, and gone home to an easier life. I have worked 2 days with chills and fever from the flu. I have had many setbacks, run out of logs, tendonitis hurting my right arm, cramps in the cold weather from pushing so hard, etc. And I do it all alone now – no one to comfort me or to be my companion. But I go step by step, and one day I'll have something. And people will say "look at him how lucky he is to have a nice cabin in the wilderness to go to and get away from the Rat Race" Lucky, Hell! I'll know how much suffering it took to get it, and how few people would have walked in my shoes.

Now getting back to you – I see an attitude developing here that we should take a look at before it grows too big. (A little seed can grow to be a mighty oak tree you know; and the bigger it gets the harder it is to cut down.) It seems you want results right now. You want to only have fun getting it, and are not willing to accept the hardship it takes to get there. Bad attitude – an express train to unhappiness. Few things ever happen like this. You must develop your mind here in a step by step manner. First you should think about what it takes to get something in competition with the rest of the people. Then you must accept this in your mind (You will not know all that it takes because your computer hasn't been fed a lot of this type of experience yet). This takes time, but you should have a track to follow that will lead to a good attitude.

You must also realize and accept the fact that that most of the time you will have to do things you don't have to do. But you must see also that "the end justifies the means." That the reward justifies the hardships. Perhaps 80% of the time people have to do things they don't like to do. Look at me now – would like to be having fun instead of all of this hardship – this is not your attitude – you say you will not do anything you don't want to do. Another bad attitude – not realistic. If you continue to believe this, then your expectations are too high for reality. And you will fight harder and harder and become more and more frustrated each time you have to do something "you don't like to do." And this will be most of the time. On the other hand if you try to be realistic about what must be done and accept it, then you will be happier not trying to live unrealistic expectations. Things will be as you expect them to be. There is also a little secret art here that I have found, and I don't think many people recognize. "There is some good in almost everything you do. No matter how bad it looks."

There is something in it for you, and something to be learned always. The art is to learn to find the good part. And to think about it as you are doing the thing you don't like to do. This will help to make you happy and will make you very accepting to most anything the world can throw at you.

Some examples of why I have talked about this and then on to another subject. These examples are only a small part and not the whole picture for what I see. You can pick each example and knock it out – it does not stand on its own – it's the whole picture I'm talking about. You were not interested in taking pictures with the cheap 35mm camera I had. I did make every effort to get a better one. And if I would have I'm sure you would have taken pictures with it. You wanted top of the line or not at all. It's OK to want the best, but when you don't have it you do the best you can with what you have. There's always something to be learned & it's better than doing nothing. You did nothing and this cheated yourself out of some learning and experience. If you could have learned to compose and take the best picture possible with the cheap camera, just think what you could do with a good one. It's the attitude you had here. A good photographer can take good pictures with a cheap camera. A poor photographer cannot take a good picture with the best camera.

2) You got bored with the cabin – It wasn't fun anymore, and you didn't want to sacrifice your summer. This is O.K. but it lacks "stick to it ness," is a selfish attitude, and you thought yourself into being unhappy. This in turn made me unhappy. And could have gotten one of us hurt. It's the attitude here. I would have never thought like this toward you. I would have wanted to help you no matter how hard it was, and no matter what else I would have liked to do because I would know that it was something you wanted and could be of help to you. If you generally love someone, you want for them what they want, and are willing to sacrifice for it. In any case I thank you for all the work you did in helping me over here – none of it was easy and you really did a lot of work.

3) You are not willing to work at any job unless it is the one you want. I think it unwise not to work at something to get a little money until you can find that job you want. <u>In the meantime keep looking</u>. A little of something is better than nothing. At least you get experience of some kind, and make a little bread even if it's not what you want. I can remember when I started with Metropolitan I was collecting nickels and dimes from people at all times of the day and night, and I had to keep going back a second and third time each month. I can also remember making $85.00 a week but never missed a payment to your mother to help for you and Lisa's support even though I had only the deer sausage that Mac brought for me to eat. I didn't like any of this and suffered for it. But I did what it took & became a manager for Metropolitan. Now I am my own Manager. I didn't start here. I've watched you around my apartment and often found you just sitting around with nothing to do. Just because you couldn't be with your friends, or whatever else you were thinking doesn't mean there isn't a 2nd best or a 3rd best thing you could do. No one can think for you about what you want to do and only you can find something interesting for you in whatever you do, and only you can keep thinking the right attitude. Everything is a habit & if you keep thinking in a good attitude, that attitude will become a habit too & you will automatically be happier. On the other hand "An idle mind is the devil's workshop." I can continue with examples, but the end result is that your attitude here is poor. I think you need to look at it here and consider some changes here. You are cheating yourself out of valuable living and happiness.

Now on to another subject. A person inherits traits from both his mother and father as well as his ancestors. Sometimes these traits work together - sometimes they work against each other. Everyone has a little of both. The problem comes when two strong traits fight with each other inside of you. Your emotions tell you that you want both traits, but they clash. I see such traits in you and they are certain to bring you unhappiness unless you are strong enough to reason them out inside of yourself and do something about them. One of these traits. (Probably inherited from your mother.) Is that you are a very social person. This is a good trait – can bring you great happiness. You must always be around people, have friends, etc. You can't stand to be alone for long. And want to share the things you do with someone. You don't want to do things alone. Now on the other hand you want to be different from everyone else. (Probably inherited from me.) This trait brings an inward happiness. One that is usually not shared with others and require a person to have great inward strength, perseverance, determination, and above all a thorough knowledge of himself. These two traits do not go together. And if you try for both of them you are sure to be unhappy. Here's why. First of all you say you are going to be different from everyone else. Let's stop a minute and look at those people who are different – there are many of them; they are different for different reasons, but they all have one thing in common. They are mostly loners. I am a little different than most, and you know me so let's take me for example. To begin with – sure I have friends, and I do some things with them. But mostly I do things alone. When I am home I spend most of the day alone. I get myself up and I go to sell insurance alone. I figure out all by myself what I will do today & how I will do it. I call on clients I never saw before and must sell them alone – no one there to help me. I do this all day. I come home and work on my pictures alone. I go on my vacations alone. Most of the time I go out in the basin or somewhere, I go alone. (Sometimes with Mac, but mostly alone). I am to finish my cabin and spend a year here alone (and I am now as alone as I have ever been.) The fact is for me though, I don't have a drive (trait) to be social as much as you do. I don't have to share all my pleasures with someone else. I would like to, but it's not necessary. I derive an inner pleasure & strength from things I do. Even if it's something I don't particularly want to do. I'll find something in it for me and I'll put it away somewhere inside of myself so it will give me a little pleasure & a little more strength.

Now there is a good reason why people who are different are loners. An all-inclusive old saying says "Birds of a feather flock together." And you can look around you and see this to be true. Rich people hang around with rich people, poor around poor, criminals around criminals, drunks around drunks, sad people around sad people. Happy people around happy people, tennis players around tennis players etc. etc. You never see a mocking bird hanging around a flock of black birds. Nor do you see a happy person hanging around *with a bunch of criminals. The reason is simple – people hang around with each other because they have something in common, can associate with each other's thoughts & ways, and they feel comfortable around each other. If you want to be different, then people can't associate with your thoughts and ways. They don't have much in common with you, and will feel uncomfortable around you. You will lose most of that "social" togetherness that as I see it <u>you can't do without</u>. Examples of this are that you complain that you have no friends. People talk to you and then leave right in the middle of a sentence, you are lost as to what to do unless you have someone to do it with, you have a strong drive to <u>impress</u> other people before impressing yourself, not satisfied with anything less than what another has (job, camera, car, etc.), and many other indications. I see these traits coupled with your emotions (will discuss later) are growing into a bigger and bigger problem. I can't see you living a life alone – you are too sociable. It is time for you to reassess these traits, and redirect your attitude. The results are only for your decision, but in view of all factors I would think your best route would be to come down to being a common person. Get with a group whose ideas you like, get yourself a girlfriend like everyone else (even if it's not exactly what you want – you must get experience with dealing with female relationships or you are in for a divorce and other troubles), get yourself a job even if it's not exactly what you want (any experience is better than nothing) <u>and keep your ideas of being different inside of you.</u> (In this way you can have all the social things you need and still think differently to yourself. This is an A #1 problem and a hard one to handle – you must give it priority.*

Now about your emotions. People are born with emotions. They are the instinctive (built in) part of us, and have an important function in preserving life. They are a very powerful force in driving a person to do a certain thing. For example; if you scare someone their emotions will trigger fear and they will run away (save themselves). If you bust someone in the mouth, their emotions will trigger anger & they will fight back (fight for themselves). Or if you are nice to them, their emotions will trigger love (take you as a friend who will help them in need) etc. Animals live almost exclusively on instinct; however their instincts are simpler than ours, and keener than ours (their very lives depend on it in a world of the survival of the fittest). An animal has little ability to reason and must make up for it in his instincts and emotions. A human being on the other hand has a relatively high ability to reason. Now if a person lives his life by emotions without using reason, like an animal, they are in for a most unhappy life (this is a guarantee). If a person goes around busting everyone in the mouth or cursing someone out every time they feel bad, or stealing something from someone else because they want it and don't feel like working for it etc. etc. then the rest of the people are not going to like that person. They will avoid him like the plague. He will have no friends, will not like himself etc. Usually these people end up mental cases if it gets bad enough, or they will end up criminals (when the seed grows into a tree) and the rest of the people will put them in a cage, just like a wild animal (my brother Richard is a good example of this). They soon begin to feel like nothing goes their way, nobody sees their ability or worth, and everything is hard for them. In the end they feel like the world owes them things so they go and take it. They not only take physical things but mental things (like they may take credit for things not due them, they will be mean to people, have little patience, always want to argue etc. Judie Mc Mahon is a good example of this) – And when a person has allowed his needs to be too great – he will have to take more than his fair share from the world. People will come down on this person and make his world an unhappy one. My theory here is that a person should first listen to his emotions. (But he shouldn't act on them yet). He should then send them through his computer and "reason" out if it's a good idea to act on those emotions. It's stupid to attack a man armed with a gun & a knife just because he made you mad by spitting on your shoe. Oftentimes you will find it not "wise" to act on an emotion. You must then learn to suppress that emotion and act on reason. People use varying degrees of emotion and reasoning – some use more emotion, some more reason. I have found that in general women act more on emotion than men. But a wise person will use "reason" before acting on emotion. This takes practice, patience and determination. Now I am talking about emotion because I see you acting on emotion to far too great an extent – and it is making you unhappy. Much of what you want is strictly emotional, and lacks reasonableness or logic. You have not learned what it takes to get something, or have not accepted the sacrifice it takes. You just blindly want it. Much of what you have had or done was given to you & you have not yet learned what efforts, money, and suffering it takes. You see what others have and you want it too. You do not see what they had to go through to get it and therefore it looks easy to you. I did not know when I started this letter, that you had taken your mother's car. I started it because of the last letter you sent me. And I could see your problems were getting the best of you. I know some *of the reasons why. It's needless of me to talk about what you did. Because you know I don't approve of any of it - nor does anyone else. But it is a good example of many things I am trying to help you with by explaining them in this letter. You are letting your emotions control you (you are not using enough reason). You are letting your needs get too great. It's wrong for you to think that anyone owes you something – why do you think someone should <u>give</u> you a car, <u>give</u> you a job like you want, <u>give</u> you money for gas. If they don't <u>give</u> it to you, you are going to <u>take</u> it. Kevin, you didn't work for these things and they are not rightfully yours. You have no right to <u>demand</u> them. If your mother gives you $10.00 for gas, she has to work 2 hours to clear this much. If someone gives you an old $200.00 truck, they still had to work many hours for it. They give these things from their heart, just as you would – it's not something they have to do. And if you demand it or take it from them, you will trigger their emotions. And they will stop giving completely – and you will find you have lost another friend. You keep on losing friends like this and others will follow. You must make an about face here. You gain much more for yourself by being nice and giving rather than taking. People realize you are just starting and this is a head point. Most are willing to help you. But this brings up something else. Would you keep giving someone a nickel if they keep throwing it away? No you wouldn't, you would soon learn their disrespect and quit. So it is with everyone else. Most people don't have enough money to buy or do the things they would like. If they give you something they bought with this money, or the money itself, they are sacrificing something they could have for themselves. If you break what they gave you, show disrespect for it, misuse it, or unwisely spend their money, they will soon learn and cut you off. Others will learn from it & cut you off. You are the one who is cutting yourself off & making yourself unhappy – <u>Not them</u>. In particular you are getting a reputation for being hard on an automobile. Sure the cars and truck were old ones. But I know too much for you, or anyone, to convince me that it was the automobile's fault. I know full well that you do not know or do not <u>respect</u> & <u>accept</u> the limits of an automobile. What bothers me is that I don't know if you are trying to learn. I have a lot to say about this, but I've already talked to you a lot about it. The results here are how people will treat you, or deal with you concerning this matter. Another complication will develop here – If you get a reputation of being hard and disrespect for an automobile. And one breaks totally because of a defect in the car, and not because of your misuse. Who do you think* *people will blame – you or the car? And so you will learn to fend society for blaming you for something you didn't do. It doesn't matter – it still causes you unhappiness – a good example of what happened to my brother Richard. <u>He was blamed for everything that happened even though he didn't do it</u>.*

Also there is another lesson to be learned here. You think everyone is honest and won't take anything from you. I've talked to you before about this & you won't come down to reality - you "throw caution to the wind." Someone stole your truck. And someone (your mother or Leo) had to work many hours for it. It's like they worked all those hours for nothing – for a criminal – a waste. You yourself stole your mother's car & almost started yourself a criminal record – think about it. People steal for many reasons just as you had yours & this truck thief had his. It doesn't matter the reason, the results are the same – and it's a reality of life.

On to another subject.

1) You are having trouble keeping your feelings steady. This is partially because of the emotions I just spoke about. You convince yourself about feeling a certain way about something or someone one day then change it entirely a short time later. Then you find yourself trying to defend yourself when someone talks to you about it. Some examples of this are last summer when you said I saved your life by taking you on the trip. Then you go home & tell everyone how you couldn't get home soon enough.

2) When you said last fall how you didn't have any friends and people who used to be your friends didn't talk to you anymore, but this summer you tell me how many people you know at school, how they all know you as "ghost writer" & how Lisa would react knowing how many friends you had.

3) Then you *said your mother was getting nicer, and all the things you would do & buy for her, yet you now won't have anything to do with her. I can go on, but you should get the picture.*

Several years ago you told me Lisa didn't want to be around me & said to you that she couldn't wait to get home from my apartment. I took her to eat at Riverside Inn & I asked her what the problem was. She said there was no problem and she didn't say that to you. I know her too well, I know the situation, you had no reason to lie, and I knew she wasn't telling me the truth. I still think it immature of her for not coming out with it so we could talk about it. Then when your mother said you told her you were counting the minutes to get away from here, you too denied it. I know you too well also, your mother had no reason to lie, and most of all I know the situation too well. You didn't even have to say it, I know already what you were thinking. And told you so one day. Often you arranged your return home with your mother on the phone. You said I was thinking too much. And I probably was, but I wasn't thinking wrong. I didn't care about this, because I know what's going on. The thing that bothers me is that this is going to cause you problems – you won't like yourself for it because you are going to have to lie to someone. You will quickly get on the wrong side of people. Also you give your mother the idea that it will be O.K. for you to have a motorcycle when I was explicit and spent a lot of time explaining to you that I do not approve of it in this day and age. And when you throw at me a statement I said about "Sometimes you have to do something dangerous just because you want to do it bad enough" it is just for argument. Such statements do not apply to everything you want. I said it in a certain context. And you know what I meant. To apply it to every situation is manipulation of reason. And not in your best interest. In any event I would think you should work on stabilizing your feelings a little better. Realize that people will do things to turn you on and off. But think about it, try to reason where they are coming from & try to set a basic feeling for them. Then if you have to say something they don't like, be able to say it to their face, and be able to have reason enough to stand your ground.

I have much more to say but for sake of time I must try to close this letter. In all that I have learned in life I find the most important thing in life is to be happy. It doesn't matter what you do in life or what you become, so long as you are happy. I have seen you become more and more unhappy with yourself & the world. I want to help you to be happier because I care. The things I say are not meant to hurt your feelings or anything else. They are meant to point out attitudes I see developing that are to be your downfall if they are allowed to get to big. I can only help by pointing them out and talking to you about them. Only you can do something about them. I talk only of the troublesome attitudes in this letter for obvious reasons. It goes without saying though that you have many good attitudes that are giving you no trouble. You are basically a good and reasonable fellow – I am proud that you are my son. Don't let a few misdirected attitudes ruin your happiness. Keep this letter and refer to it from time to time. Chances are if things aren't going your way and you are unhappy you may find something in it that could help you.

Sun 10/11/81

Fitted the two 25' logs and put pins in them to straighten them out. These are the last 25 footers. The next ones over these will be the roof supports. Peeled a 20' log and set it atop cabin. The Dziuk's logs came in yesterday – may need a couple before I am finished. Need at least a 20 footer. Peeled logs for a couple of hours by lantern light. Tenderness a little better today. Hope this is a sign it is going away. Have been taking 2600 mg. of aspirin per day and 4 one a day vitamins. Didn't rain but looked stormy (like snow) all day.

Mon. 10/12/81

Fitted log over back window. Peeled others for gable ends until John Dziuk came in from work. Went to his place and drug over a 20' log for the front (last one) and a few smaller ones for the gable ends. Peeled the 20 footer and set it on top the cabin by lantern light. The day was overcast, but tonight it seems to be clearing – Moon is bright – temp is a cool 20° shortly after dark. I've the last few days that all the larch trees are now turning yellow – They seem to cover the mountainside. Up till now only the broad leaf trees have turned yellow.

The North Fork of the Flathead River

Tues. 10/13/81

Went for mail and to make phone calls. Fitted 20' log over front of cabin – last 20 footer. Hoisted a roof support log (30') on top of cabin on top of cabin. Went to Costello's and Brown's to see if they wanted anything in town. We get into town so seldom (especially me) that we have to check with each other. Left chain saw at Dziuk's and went to the "answer auction" in Kalispell. I am looking for skis. No skis my size
– bought some badly needed leather gloves, pencils and a few tools. Went to Hotel, but couldn't get to sleep until just before daylight. I've been sleeping in the tent (with one ear open and a gun by my pillow) so long that I expect to hear coyotes howl, elk bugle, deer hoof on the ground, ravens call etc. that the street noises disorient me and keep me awake.

Wed. 10/14/81

Went to pick up hand saw I had sharpened, get supplies, food, wash clothes, get snowmobile title, make phone calls etc. I looked at myself in a full length mirror at the motel. I am as skinny as a rail. Must get that cabin up so I can slack off work, and begin eating better. Spent all day in the towns. Back to camp just before dark. Picked up my chain saw and talked to John Dziuk about the construction of his house (he is just starting). Went to Costello's to bring some chain saw parts I picked up for him. Ate and went to Hostel to sit down and write letters. Spent most of the time talking to guest. Picked up food I had ordered

Thurs. 10/15/81

Put up the 2 first roof logs (and last wall logs) and fitted and rodded them. Cut the other 30 footer to length. Went to Hostel for shower and to write the letter I didn't get to write yesterday.

Photo of the North Fork Road

Frank Even's Outhouse

Fri 10/16/81
To Polebridge to get mail and make phone calls. Peeled 2 logs to start gable ends. These are the last wall logs to be notched. Worked all day on fitting one – a troublesome one.

Sat. 10/17/81

Decided today to try to put the gable ends together on the ground rather than working up the wall. Peeled a couple logs, and fitted 5 of the gable logs together. Frank Evans, the guy who writes the article "Up the North Fork" in the Hungry Horse newspaper came by today. Just wanted to talk. Said he mentioned in his article that I was building a cabin. After dark I peeled 2 more logs (They are smaller than the big wall logs and go faster). And cut 30' of ¾" steel rod into 17" pieces for securing the logs. Weather was nice today – sunshine and high about 50°. The tenderness is better in my arm – will try to get off those aspirin before they eat out my stomach. Feel better about things today. Can see where I can move faster now, and getting to where I can see a roof on soon. Elk began bugling again last night. One big one was right near the camp – nearly scared me out of my sleeping bag.

Sun 10/18/81

Another pretty day, but cold – high 20's. Warmed up during the day though. Fitted the last notched log over the back of the cabin and took it down. Put it on the jig and fitted the other side to the gable logs. Fitted more gable logs together. Went to Dziuk's to get 2 more logs. Peeled them after dark – till 10 p.m. Went to the Hostel for a hot bath and stopped by the spring to fill up water jugs.

Mon 10/19/81

Awakened by Chuck Dziuk – Their truck battery was down and it wouldn't start. Boosted their battery and got them going. Finished fitting logs for back gable and cut them across the ends and put some of them on the cabin. Can't work this high anymore without a scafflold of some kind. Gable ends too wobbly now, and dangerous to climb on them. Took gable apart and set it aside. Set other logs on gig to begin the other gable end. Quit about 10:30 or 11:00. Good weather today, so put in a long day.

Tues 10/20/81

Got up late today. Was tired last night from long day and wind kept making noises around the tent. About 5:00 a.m. another elk let out a hair-raising bugle right below the bluff. These things can be heard for miles from across the river in Glacier Park, and when one is right on you the noise is exceptionally loud. He kept this up every 5 minutes or so for about ½ hour. Went to Polebridge for mail and phone calls. Stopped by to talk to H. Frank Evans about ordering some cashew nuts and ended up eating there. He showed me around his place and talked for an hour or more. He is 70 years old (10 days ago he said) and is quite a character and a pleasant guy. Nearly 2 p.m. before I got back to camp. Weather was 30° or so but the wind was biting. Cut a log and made a scaffold for the back gable. Set 3 more logs up there. Began fitting the last notched log on the front wall – didn't quite finish by dark. Too windy to work after dark so I quit – the cold (now 28°) is not so bad, but even a slight wind makes it more than uncomfortable. By the time I ate and began taking a bath the temp was 24°. I've noticed lately that after the initial shock of being out in this temp stark naked, it is not so bad as it was when I first began taking baths out in it. It seems my body is adjusting somehow to tolerate the cold.

Wed. 10/21/81 Just as I was thinking I was adjusting to the cold, the temperature drops to 8°. I was cold even in my sleeping bag. Was tired – too tired to sleep; animals outside making all sorts of noises. Finally I got up and put one sleeping bag inside of the other. Went to sleep just before daybreak. Up late a.m. – Ice on logs. Needed active work to keep warm, so I took the chain saw down the bluff and cut down all the dead lodgpole pine in front of the 2 lots and whatever was in the way of the

John & Joyce O'Hara's Outhouse
(1940 Model)

view. Took about 3 hours. Came up and fitted (finished) log over front of cabin. Took it down to fit it on next gable log on gig. Went to Dziuk's to get another 8" log. Talked about hunting this Sunday (beginning of season). They were about to eat and talked me into staying for supper. It was dark when I left and getting cold fast. Went to the Hostel to soak in the bathtub and to begin a Halloween card for Pat and her kids. Didn't do much on cabin today.

Thurs 10/22/81

Chuck Dziuk came by – their truck wouldn't start again and needed a boost. Went down to start their truck and pulled a log over from their house. Peeled and fit it on one of the gable logs. Worked on the gable all day – finished about ½ of it. Mr. Gene? Kennedy who owns 2 lots between me and the Brown's came over and talked a while.

Fri. 10/23/81

Went to Polebridge to get mail, write to Mac, and make phone calls. Talked to Mom for a good while today – also Kevin seems to be more contented with things. Spent the day hauling lumber for roof decking and floor (subfloor) from the Lee Downes' place to the cabin. Bent the tailgate on the truck from

too much weight. Don't know if it can be fixed – it won't close. Went to supper at Karen Feather's place (Polebridge Store). She had also invited Rich and Wendy Upton. He is a character. Enjoyed the company and also doing something different. Started the Dziuk's truck again this morning – they need a new battery.

The North Fork of the Flathead River

Sat 10/24/81

Straightened tailgate on truck – took most of the morning, but was able to salvage it. Worked on cabin. Tom Sluiter a neighbor from across the valley came over and visited a while. Invited me to dinner. Sighted in rifle for hunting season – opens tomorrow. Went to dinner with Tom and Ginny. Back to camp around midnight. I feel bad today. Have some sort of intestinal problem that has been with me for about 3 weeks now. It's getting worse and today I have chills and fever.

Sun. 10/25/81

Up at 6:00 a.m. Climbed down the bluff and walked to the river before daylight. Waited for a couple of hours in case a deer or elk might try to cross from Glacier Park. Looked around the rest of the morning – very little sign of either deer or elk in the area. Went back and worked on the cabin. Frank Evans came by just to talk. Asked me to stop by his house tonight and have dinner with him. All these dinner invitations all of a sudden – the word must be getting out that I'm not eating right or something. Went to Polebridge store for gas. Karen Feather asked me if I felt alright. I must look sick too. I told her I had chills and fever but was O.K. She wanted me to stay at the store where it was warmer. Went to Hostel for shower; to Frank Evans for dinner and to visit. Getting to like the guy more and more. He is 70 years old but quite spirited and active. Went to Polebridge store about 9:30 p.m. and spent the night there. Chills and fever now more pronounced and the glands on my upper legs are very swelled. I must now have an infection somewhere.

Monday 10/26/81

Rainey today and I feel bad. Stayed at the store and played with a little cube game all day. A friend of Karen's mother was there and picked an argument with Karen's Mother. Karen took her to the airport in Kalispell after insisting she leave. This was about 11:00 a.m. – this was a bad scene. I stayed up with Bettie (Karen's Mother) till 1:30 a.m. & then went to bed – Fever and chills still with me.

Tues. 10/27/81

Couldn't sleep last night – got up late. I can't seem to shake the fever and chills. Decided to see a doctor today. Took pictures of a generator for Karen. Took a fellow named Frank up to Spruce Creek to his trailer on the way to town. Stopped by McDonald Creek to talk to Rangers about taking pictures of the eagles there. Went to doctor's office in Whitefish. He couldn't figure out what was causing my problem. Gave me a prescription to try and if it didn't work within 1 week, he would refer me to a specialist. Went to auction in Kalispell. Bought a few tools, Sally Costello and Jane Brown were there. Had coffee with them and talked till midnight.

Wed 10/28/81

Washed clothes, bought supplies, groceries etc. and made several phone calls. Spent several hours on the phone. Got to Polebridge about 9:30 p.m. It sure seems to get dark early and not much time in the day. Feel only slightly better today. Stayed at Polebridge store for the night.

Picture: From left to right,
Jerry & Sally Costello, Jane & Sam Costello, and little Kimmy

Thurs. 10/29/81

Up 6:30 a.m., already getting daylight with time change (Sunday night). Went hunting up Red Meadow Road. Having difficulty walking so I did a lot of sitting and riding around in the truck. Jumped a deer, but he was downwind and he saw me before I saw him. Came back to camp a while and drove to Hay Creek Rd. Hunted in an

open field until dark – nothing! Went to Polebridge store and had dinner there. Ron and D'Ann Wilhelm joined us. Stayed for the night. It's warmer and more comfortable at the store. But I miss not hearing the sounds of the animals at night.

Fri 10/30/81

Up 6:00 a.m. went hunting in the open field off Hay Creek Rd. – again nothing! To Polebridge 10:00 a.m. to make phone calls. Worked on the cabin rest of the day. Went to the Polebridge store 7 p.m. where I had supper with Karen and her mother and 3 of the Park Service people.

Outhouse in Polebridge Meadow

Sat. 10/31/81

Up 5:30 a.m. and to Apgar bridge in Glacier Park to photograph eagles. Just about daylight the eagles began coming in – about 270 of them by Park Service count. The weather clouded up and started sprinkling. I stayed for a couple of hours and watched, but decided I would come on a better day. And

so didn't take a picture. Many ducks and seagulls in the area also. The eagles are attracted by the Kokanee salmon that come from Flathead Lake and spawn there. The waters are full of fish. In some areas they are so thick they obscure the bottom of the crystal clear McDonald Creek. Came back to Polebridge and slept for an hour or two. Went to camp

and worked on cabin till dark. Back to Polebridge and attended a Halloween masquerade party at the Northern Lights Saloon. Everyone dressed to the theme "Enemies of the North Fork". It was a good show. Went hunting at the end of Whale Creek Rd. all day. Jumped a deer and after dark, as I was coming out of the mountains, I jumped what sounded like an elk. Too dark to see

Sun 11/1/81

Went Hunting at the end of Whale Creek Road all day. Jumped a deer. And after dark, as I was coming out of the mountains, I jumped what sounded like an elk. It was too dark to see.

Mon. 11/2/81

Woke up late – thick fog this morning. Worked on the cabin all day. Finished gable ends and put half of it up. Raised a purlin log and fitted it in place. Raised the other but didn't have time to fit it before dark. Went to the Dziuk's to salt down two deer skins and an elk skin I got from them. To Polebridge to eat and sleep.

Tues. 11/3/81

Up 5:00 a.m. Picked up Perry Dziuk (John's brother) and went hunting at the end of Whale Creek Rd. Neither of us saw anything all day, But there was some fresh deer and elk sign. Got back after dark. Stayed at Polebridge store. Tonight I'm tired – didn't sleep much last night.

Wed. 11/4/81

Got up at daylight, but still sleepy. Went back to bed and got up at 9:30 a.m. Called Helen and Mom and worked on the cabin the rest of the day. Worked on fitting the purlin logs in place. Perry Dziuk came over to take pictures of the cabin. Stayed at Polebridge store.

Thurs 11/5/81
Spent the day taking pictures of the eagles along McDonald Creek in Glacier
Park. Some 400 of them there now. The day was pretty but cool. Stayed at
Polebridge store.

Fri. 11/6/81
Spent the morning on the phone. Chopped some firewood for the store. Worked on the cabin the rest of the day. The logs on the top were icy all day. A very slippery and dangerous condition – must use care on days like this. Stayed at Polebridge store. Temp 6° last night.

Sat. 11/7/81
Worked on the cabin all day. One gable end finished. The other needs only the 2 logs at the peak. Then the ridgepole will go on. Logs icy all day today. Very slippery and difficult to work on. Frank Evans came over today. Stayed at Polebridge store.

Sun 11/8/81
Worked on finishing other gable end. Spent all afternoon bracing the gables and trying to get the ridgepole up. Put up logs over purlin strips to use as a catwalk, but by days end was still not able to get the ridgepole all the way up and in place. This one is really pushing me – very difficult for me to handle alone. Stayed at Polebridge store.

Bill & Jane Brown's horse "Outlaw" with grizzly bear behind him

Mon. 11/9/81

Cut down some lodgepole pine to begin making rafters. Spent 3 hours or so getting the ridgepole in place after the frost had burned off. Bettie from the Polebridge store came by to take pictures of the cabin while I was feeding the horses at Costello's. Visited with Frank Evans for a while after dark. He showed me how to make an elk bugle. Mac called yesterday. Joan had a 5 lb. 14 oz. baby girl. Named it Renee; also said the tenants in the house in Lafayette have moved out. Talked to Helen and Mrs. Hurst about the house and tried to call the tenants.

Tues. 11/10/81

Spent an hour or so on the phone taking care of the rental house and talking to Mom. Cut up most of the extra logs and in general cleaned up the area around the cabin so I could work better. Peeled 7 lodgepoles for rafters. To the store to make call at 4:30 p.m., fed Costello's horses. Stayed at Polebridge store.

Wed 11/11/81

Up at daylight and went walking below the cabin. Jumped some ducks and a deer. The deer was too far away and running through timber. Couldn't tell if it was a buck or a doe. Cut more lodgepoles on Dziuk's property – maybe these won't have as much taper as the ones on the bluff. Peeled lodgepoles until dark. The sky was overcast and the moonlight wasn't bright enough to peel logs, so I stacked the rest of the firewood I had cut. Showered at the Hostel and stayed at the store.

Thurs 11/12/81

A cold rainy day today. Cut more lodgepoles on Dziuk's property and peeled until dark. It gets dark so early, especially when it is cloudy – about 5:00. Have about 20 of the 36 rafters I need. The weather today is different. The clouds over the mountains are low and dense, and white with a sharp lower line. Perhaps snow is to fall soon. Have also noticed lately that there seems to be a scarcity of animals. Deer haven't been around for a couple of months now. All the little ground squirrels disappeared about that time also. The chipmunks have been out of sight for about 2 weeks now. Don't see or hear

many tree squirrels. Haven't herd the elk for a couple of weeks. The coyotes however, have become more active. When I hunt there seems to be little animal sign of any kind. Perhaps most of the big game have gone to Glacier Park. The pretty yellow trees are all brown now. The water in the streams are flowing slower now. It is all a big change from when I came here in July. Also noticed the birds are different. More eagles around, no more hummingbirds, more "camp robbers," an unfamiliar large brown bird is around, & fewer ravens. Visited Costellos after dark and had tacos with them – talked about hunting. Stayed at Polebridge store.

Fri. 11/13/81
Spent the morning taking care of business on the phone. Mom seems to be doing O.K., my house will be rented today, Larry Hurst to visit me here Sun., a week, Kevin doing O.K. Began to snow heavily around noon. Snowflakes an inch in diameter are falling. Peeled more lodge pole today. It is cold and wet. The snow covers the ground but is wet. It makes the logs muddy, the snow stopped about an hour before dark and the sky cleared over the mountains, black clouds above them, and white fog in the valley below. A beautiful sight. My camera is at the Polebridge store for the first time today – It'll stay in the truck from now on. Stayed at the Polebridge store.

Sat 11/ 14/ 81

Woke up to about 2 inches of snow this morning. Decided to go hunting and take advantage of tracking while the snow was still on the ground. As I was leaving the Polebridge store, a station wagon (4 wheel drive) backed up into the side of my truck and pushed in the right side of my rear quarter panel. The owner was Leo McDonald – he just didn't see me. We called the highway patrol, but they couldn't come way out here to make a report. They will mail me forms to fill out. We exchanged names and I got the name of his insurance carrier. I am fast getting what is known up here as a "North Fork truck." Went hunting along the river below the cabin. Not much sign of animals. Picked up a large deer track and trailed him till dark. He went about 3 miles. Didn't see it. I look at the snow covered trees and think – we try to make our Christmas trees this pretty by spraying on an artificial snow. But here are the real God made Christmas trees – and thousands of them – it is beautiful. It makes me more aware that man can't duplicate the hand of God. Came back to Polebridge store wet and cold. Frank Evans came over, and he Bettie Jacobsen and I had an enjoyable supper. Stayed at the store for the night.

Sun 11/15/81

Up at daylight and went over to Frank Evans' house. He wasn't up yet. We had some of his homemade huckleberry pancakes and then towed his truck into Columbia Falls. The road was icy and snowy. It took us over 2 hours. We returned about noon. Went to camp and cut down 7 more lodgepoles and peeled 6 of them before dark. It began snowing again just before dark. Came to Polebridge store – Sally Costello invited me over to their house for supper and to watch a movie on T.V. with some of their friends. Ate supper with Bettie Jacobsen and went to Costellos' for a couple of hours. Stayed at the store.

Mon 11/16/81

Worked on rafters all day. Frank Evans came by to bring me a hand saw for cutting the roof decking. Didn't snow today – snow on the ground was wet and soggy. Heard an elk bugle today, first time in several weeks that I heard one. Stayed at the Polebridge store. Helen called tonight. Kevin broke the back window of her car, messed up the trailer and left home.

Tues 11/17/81

Woke up to 4 or 5 inches of snow. Called Helen, Mom, and Mike Norse. Mike will arrange to have one of the counselors at the Sherriff's office talk to Kevin. Don't know if this will help, but Kevin will soon end up in trouble with the law, and I can't think of much else to do. Guess he will just have to learn things the hard way - he seems to have trouble thinking them out. Got a letter from him today, he seems so mixed up. Stopped by Frank Evans' place to pick up a ladder and had lunch with him. Went to work on the cabin in heavy snowstorm. Needed chains to get up Vance Hill. Nearly 18 inches of snow around cabin. The weight of the snow had collapsed the tent. Worked on fitting rafters, but work was slow and icy. Fitted 4 rafters by dark and started another. Stayed at the store.

Dad.

I just put down your book (letter) and practically everything I've
known from the begining and had it programmed on the ole
commputer all the time, all I needed to was for someone
to help me press the "enter" button.

J'm in a good mood (now for the last couple of days)
despite moma & leo's fighting. This letter will be a little
confusing & unorderly and a little dusty with the
pen (J had to give of something in this dept. for the Art talent).

to start off some of the things Jill tell you probably
won't make any sense telling you.

One thing, One, thing, One thing, One thing,.... is moma &
leo are fighting about money —stupid— she's mad cause
he doesn't make enough and she's got to support him.
If you love someone money doesn't mean zilch!
In today's society women are equal now, and they
should have been all along, so what difference should
it make who wins the bread in the family. There are
plenty of families who's wife brings home the bacon.
the fact is your not marrying for their job but because
you want to be with them. now J could have told anyone
mom & leo wouldn't last 3yrs (and J did) and she just
told him not to come back (jost like she told me!)
she jost wanted to get married, have someone at home,
she didn't care about love. she kept telling everyone "J
just wish hed go away, he's silly and stupid"
now Jue learned two things ① money doesn't mean a thing
                                    in love
                          ② marry someone for thamselves

yes, I'm in a good mood, but not totally happy. to be happy I have to be able to look back at the things I've accomplished within + without myself and be proud.

About my job... the best job in the world! I'm an apprentice for a sign maker. I work after school till about 5 + sat + sun. I get $40 a wholeday + $20 ½. he's also a diesel, electric engineer and goes out on rigs about once or twice a month for a day and I can go too. I'd make 1 to 2 hundred + a free helicopter ride.. The man I work for is named Frank Addison, An old man. He used to be a big man with a lot of money but he's to old now. he gave his rigs, cranes + money all away to his kids + grand kids. He didn't know how good I painted but today I painted the side of a big 3 ton truck And says I'll paint the signs so he can go onto other things + business will go faster, so I'll be in more loot pretty soon.

Mom told me to come back home now. so I'ts easy to get to work.

He's done stuff like Al George Inc. Monosep. Petroleum Helicopters, Acadiana mall, etc.

my bike,
I'm paying for a bike mom bought for me last
$140 night + have paid $60 already. you were right about me being obnoxious about having things been given to me + not taking care of them. I've bought that radio + my bike and havent let either one out of my sight I'ts a pretty bike, Murray dirt bike but "big" for road also. Just the thing for someone as hard on bikes as I'. I keep in in my room and I've thought about it a lot.

187

I haven't seen anyone with a bike like this before so you know this makes me happy. this is one of the thing I've thought about I can't tell if it's an "ego" problem or not, maybe you can tell me? every one like it And I can't wait to let everyone ride it. I even Almost let lisa take if for the night ?! Old @ #. I've completely forgot about a car. that's just somethin till I save some money for A down payment.

pause: It's for certain he's going. when he just packed his truck and gave her the house key and she laughing.

I'm glad you've told me about conflicting traits. I couldn't figure it out for anything. for ex: I'd wait all morning just to go sit out on the playground with all my friends, but when I'd get out there, I'd think what am I doing here, I feel like I don't belong and if someone says something to me I'll answer them and rush off.
   I've also noticed that without mark I've really no good friends at all. At school it's a strong relationship and even a strong love for A couple of my girl-friends. Marks my best friend but he works too much, I never see him; at school I've really 1 or 2 of guy's I talk a lot to in class And about 10 girls in each class. but on the weekend I've know one to share my time with. when we have a game I'm constantly walking around just stoping to talk for a second to talk, like I'm in a hurry. There's no one to sit with or go do something with. I think the problem is all of my girl-friends or any body I hang around with at school are too popular for me. Joh just made homecoming queen & shanna 1st maid.

so it's kind of subconciencly I'm thinking why would they want to spend their time with me or how would it look for me to be seen with them. I thought it might be an Inferiority complex. All through school I've kind of been an out cast since I was larger than anyone else. up until high school, I didn't know what a girl was, but I had lots of friends then. Scoot chris, oscar, mark lerrell. All weekend we couln't find time to do everything. every weekend was spending the night over.

I still am very self concious •
=

I've also except ed my falts that I can see. ① is my stretching of the truth - trying to impress! ② lack of concentration ③ lack of will power. these are just off the top of my head i tell me more of them, the sooner the better! !!!.

you often here people say - " he died doing what he liked best" If I die, no matter what age, that will be written on my tombstone.

I have a strong sense of daring + wanting to do things dangerously. whe I do something dangerous it makes me feel like 5 yrs of life have been added to me. for a while I wanted to be a stunt man. I like to jump from high places, jump ramps with cars, bikes but not motocycles I have Ideas for a lot of stunts, some I'm ready for right now and even planned one for the old track. there's so many things I want to do with a car!

now my answer to you about the motocycle was " I'll be doing dangerous things in my life" your write about that being different. riding a motorcycle for years is dangerous but wouldn't give me the feeling as jumping

through a hoop of fire in a $150 car. but I have a
strong curiosity of just riding one for a little while.
I will have one later on in life because I think
it's safe enough for at least highways. And riding
one for a long time down a highway is where I think
the fun is. I've swallowed your every word and
plenty of others too. And I too have come to the
conclusion that motorcycles are not good for everyday
riding. but everytime I see one the curiosity gets
stronger, that's why I'm thinking of buying a new one.
you've seen it at the snow cat place. the kawasaki
250 or better as david has told me. when I sat on
it it was a feeling I'm still not familiar with.
I just want one to satisfy that feeling, to ride to
dallas, or to florida, or grand mahales, not in a city
if I can help it. there's one thing I want to know...
what did you tell grandpa when he said he didn't want
you having one?

10/24
It's been a week or so since I wrote
the above + things are changing, my attitudes
changing. It just turned cold And the old man
isn't working worth a damn. I've been sitting
here for 6 days without working. I started
looking for another job. I talked him into
letting me work tomorrow + this weekend I'm
working with chris too. I'm still in the hole with
gas + I need to pay david too.

I think Lafayette is not a good place for me, I feel like I don't belong, I feel strongly about this. I think about saving money and moving away to California a lot. David ~~thinks~~ doesn't think it's a good idea me staying with mom A. He almost thinks I should have stayed in Dallas like we were thinking. There is a little saying that fate has been telling me lately" Just when you think you can make ends meet, someone moves an end!

I've been checking around about motorcycles, ~~some~~ some more. There ARE still people telling me it's crazy to get one, but people still think it's a good idea to get one too! I've got a booklet on them from the Drivers license place and I also talked to one policeman (old) and he sayd If you don't take chances and keep a good head about them, driving defensive, be ready to stop, watch out for the other guy, then it's just like any thing else. A friend down the street has a honda 350, I got it running for him so he lets me ride it. I ride every day, trying to teach myself how to ride... I've got a lot to learn. Dad I'll never stop thinking about it & looking for information. I'm going to be positive about it the day I buy it. I've been hearing both sides, and will never stop hearing, And they even themselves out so I kind of leaving it up to my judgement.

191

Right now I'm going for it, but I could change my mind! I will listen to anything more you have to say to me, but I'll tell ya, I will have one some time in my life, and I need to learn alot about it, can you tell me what you know. I'm having trouble starting off, slow with the clutch, braking and what size bike to get. If you can't talk me out of it, can you atleast help me from breaking my neck or leg.

You've been giving me advice about your experiences, David too. I think you rode too crazy, standing up, wheelies, jumping tracks, I don't care what you tell me about after I get one, I ain't doing those things. Besides, didn't grandpa tell you he didn't want you having one. I just want to ride, I just met some friends that want me to ride with the, these couple of guys are really level headed and come from the good side of the tracks.

I hear you're feeling bad, dad, don't push yourself It's just a cabin compared to your life & health!
I'll stop for now, I hope you try to understand about the bike.

I love you dad
Kevi

193

Wed. 11/18/81
Hunted all day around Coal Creek. Saw fresh deer tracks in the snow, but no elk sign. Found a small deer rub near a secluded meadow. It was a strange rub though. It appears the deer stripped a ½" branch with his teeth and then bit it off. Then he scratched the ground and left. Late in the evening I followed another deer track to a deer rub on the side of the North Fork Rd. – of all places to have a rub, this one was used by three deer since the snow last night. I watched it till dark—nothing. I'll watch it again in the morning--- It looks like a good one. Went back and stayed at the store. Karen Feather returned today from her trip to Arizona.

Thurs. 11/19/81
Went to watch the deer rub before daylight. Saw a coyote (big one) but no deer. Returned to store to eat breakfast about 11a.m. Worked on cabin the rest of the day. Didn't snow during the day, but the icy logs really slow me down. Back to store after dark

Fri. 11/20/81

Spent the morning on the phone with Willie and Helen, wrote letters, then went to work on the cabin. I finished notching rafters on the north side and started cutting rafters for the south side. Still too icy to secure rafters to ridgepole and pearlin strip. Stayed at the Polebridge store tonight.

Sat. 11/21/81

To Kalispell to get supplies, see about picking up snowmobile. Also went to ski sale and bought a couple of old skis and poles. Couldn't find cross country skis, which is what I came here for. Went to ski party at the Outlaw Inn. Stayed at the Blue and White Motel.

Sun. 11/22/81

Went to Northwest Sports and waxed the snowmobile, washed clothes and did a little shopping. Cleaned out the truck and went to the airport to pick up Larry Hurst. Called Mac from the airport. Larry came in at 8:45 p.m. on schedule. We stayed at the Blue and White Motel.

Mon. 11/23/81

Had breakfast and went to the Ford dealer to get an estimate on truck damage. Went to get the snowmobile. Really had to pack things since we already had a truck full of stuff. Snow is starting to fall. We went through Glacier Park to see the eagles. The government went broke Friday and so the regular park employees weren't on duty—so I took Larry to the researchers blind. There were two girls (researchers') in the blind so we left. They radioed the rangers and I was issued a $25.00 ticket. We did break the rules, but the fine did not fit the crime. The road through the park was closed so we had to backtrack, and take another road. The road was slippery and we had to drive slowly. We got to Polebridge in the middle of the afternoon. Larry had brought a large ice chest full of seafood, most of which we put in a freezer drawer in Kalispell. We had shrimp etouffee for supper. I had made arrangements for Larry and I to stay at the Polebridge store for the week and we would supply the food.

Tues 11/24/81

Went to camp by late morning - showed Larry around. He was impressed by the view and anxious to work on the cabin. We spent the day securing the rafters and getting them ready for the decking. The logs were icy and slippery.

Temperature, in the twenties. Larry wasn't used to the temperature and was cold. He just needs to get a little acclimatized and perhaps some wool clothing. I had gotten word that Costello wanted to see me. We went to his house after dark. He was leaving for a month and wanted me to stay in his cabin to look after

things and feed his horses. I agreed to stay there starting Monday. Went to the store and had Ragu spaghetti sauce and venison over rice for supper.

Wed. 11/25/81
Larry and I worked on the cabin until dark. Temperature in the teens today --- We built a fire to warm up by. At dark I went over to Costello's to go over the things he wanted me to do while he was gone. Went to Polebridge and had oyster soup. Went to the saloon to see a movie (Caine Mutiny). The community got together and will show a movie once a month this winter.

Bettie, Larry & Karen
inside of the Polebridge Store

Larry on the pay phone (in the barrel)
outside of the Polebridge Store

Thurs. 11/26/81

Began decking the northwest side of the roof today. Larry decked while I worked on fitting the rafters on the south east side. We quit around 3:00 p.m. To go to the thanksgiving supper at the Community Hall up the road about 8 miles. We took a pot of crawfish etouffee that Larry brought from La., and a pecan pie that Karen had baked. There were about 50 people there, and they all brought their favorite dish - it was a feast. We came back to the store and taught Karen and Bettie how to play bourre – "she took us for a ride".

Fri. 11/27/81

Larry and I took the snowmobile up to Trail Creek near the border to learn to ride it. We also planned to hunt from it. The road had ruts in it and we took several spills before we learned to handle it. We took turns riding alone at first. We then doubled up and took a gun with us. We intended on doing some hunting, but concentrated most of our time on watching the road and trying to keep our balance. We stopped to follow a couple of elk tracks, but had too much clothing on for walking up the mountain. We put about 30 miles on the snowmobile and got back to camp around 6:00 p.m., fed Costello's horses and lit a fire in his stove. The temperature was -5°

Photo of USA & Canadian Border. Trees cut to form the dividing line.

Last night and didn't warm up much during the day. Stopped by Tom and Genny Sluter's for a few minutes and then to Polebridge store. Karen and Bettie had the rest of the crawfish etouffee. Larry and I went to Frank Evans' cabin for supper. He had some of his friends over. We had roast pork with trimmings and some of his apple dumplings for desert. Had roseptal and elderberry wine that frank had made. Took pictures in his cabin. He gave Larry a bottle of his homemade wine to take home to La. - we were both tired.

The snowmobile tires you, like riding offshore in a boat. You expend a lot of energy moving back and forth and side to side to keep yourself upright.

Photos inside of Frank Evens' cabin
Jerry & Sally Costello's Horses

Sat. 11/28/81

We got up and made shrimp gumbo for tonight's supper. Worked on the cabin all day. At dark we went to the Costello's to feed horses. Unloaded the snowmobile as I was going to leave it here while I stayed in his cabin. We had invited Frank Evans over for supper. The gumbo was excellent. We all enjoyed the food and each other's company. We packed Larry's things in the truck and drove to Kalispell – Stayed at the Blue and White Motel.

Photo of Jerry & Sally Costello's Cabin above
Photo of James Hale (The Cajun Mountain Man) Below

Sun. 11/29/81

Up at 5:30 a.m. to eat and take Larry to the airport. He seemed to have enjoyed the week here – hope he did. His plane left at 7:05 a.m. I drove back to the North Fork and hunted the rest of the day – no luck! Today is the last day of hunting season. I'm disappointed that I didn't get either a dear or an elk.

First year I scratched on deer since I began hunting big game nearly 20 years ago. It just doesn't seem right for me to scratch in the middle of big game country. Ron Wilhelm had supper with us at the store. Stayed at the store tonight.

Mon 11/30/81
Packed all my belongings in the truck as I was to stay at the Costello's tonight & for a while. Chopped firewood for Karen for an hour or so. We then went to Frank Evan's land to get slabs of wood for both Frank and Karen. The slabs were from a portable sawmill. We spent the afternoon doing this. Had gumbo for supper.

Went to Costello's to tend to his place and sleep there. Talked to Helen and Kevin this morning. Kevin is staying in Dallas with David. He is working at a fast food place. He has quit school and wanted to talk to me about taking the GED exam. Helen has also taken a second job driving a hotshot truck. Larry had brought a bunch of cookies, fruitcake, candy Etc. that Mom had made & fudge that Mrs. Landry had made. It's been a real treat all week. Still have a lot of it left.

Photo of Costello's barn (Burnt down in the 1988 Red Bench Fire)

Tues 12/1/81
Wrote letters this morning and went to Polebridge for my mail. Pat sent me a package of 2 shirts and a Rubik's cube for my birthday. I also got a box of excellent photographic images and instructions (books) from the Hurst's'. Got stuck in the snow trying to get in my driveway. Frank Spitall's came over to see my cabin and helped me get out. He is also trying to get a roof on his cabin. Fitted 7 rafters by dark. John Dziuk plowed the road today – shouldn't get stuck again until next hard snow. Guess I'll have to put the chains on and leave them on. Went to the store and had dinner (supper) with Karen and Bettie. Mac called while I was there. I stayed at the Costello's' cabin.

Wed. 12/2/81

Woke up to a heavy snowstorm. Had to use the snowmobile to get to the cabin. Worked till late evening. Before the storm subsided there was over a foot more snow on the ground. I dropped my tape measure somewhere in the snow and couldn't find it. Went to the truck to get another one just as the sun was peeking through. I got

my camera and took a couple of pictures. Took the Dziuks' kids riding on the snowmobile. Johnna wanted me to show her how to ride it. She will be 7 on Dec. 5th – same as my birthday. I rode with her and let her drive. I was amazed that she wasn't afraid of the throttle and had the strength to handle it. Worked until dark fitting the rafters. John Dziuk plowed the road in the dark. It took him 4 hours instead of the usual 1 hour because the snowmobile packed the snow. From now on I'll run on a little strip on the side of the road.

Thurs. 12/3/81

Spent half the morning rounding up the horses. One had gotten out over the fence in the barn and had stepped on the snowmobile – only scratched it

fortunately. When I opened the gate to get it in, the other 4 got out, also. Worked on the rafters today. The Dziuk kids came over and wanted to ride the snowmobile again. I didn't want to quit work, but told them I would get off before dark and come down to their place. When I got there they were punished and couldn't ride the snowmobile. I drove down to the store on the snowmobile for the first time. I gave it a little more throttle on the open road, and in no time was up over 50 M.P.H. This thing has more power than I suspected. A car couldn't match the acceleration with good traction, and certainly couldn't match the

speed on icy road. Had supper with Karen and Bettie. They told me I wasn't supposed to run the snowmobile on the North Fork Rd. So many rules and regulations everywhere you go. I can see this should apply on busy roads, but up here in the middle of nowhere, I can't see that it should make much difference. Anyway, I'm going to do it until someone stops me.

Fri 12/4/81

Up before daylight this morning – have been waking up before daylight every day for a while now. Had breakfast, fed the horses and went up to Polebridge to call Kathlyn Hurst. She will fly to Kalispell Sunday – all is O.K. Wrote

letters to the U.S. Magistrate in Kalispell and the Hungry Horse news about the fine I got in Glacier Park. Went to D'Ann Wilhelm's to pick up 25 lbs. of cashews Frank Evans and I ordered. To frank Evans' house and then to work on the cabin. Worked for about 3 hours on the rafters and then to Dziuk's about ½ hour before dark. I had promised to let them ride the snowmobile to Polebridge after dark for supper with Karen, Bettie and Tom Riemer. I'm not supposed to run the snowmobile on the North Fork Road so I've been careful to run at night or when few people are out. Ran the speedometer to 65 M.P.H. on the icy North Fork road tonight. A car could never catch me on this thing – still didn't use full throttle. Got a very disturbing letter from Pat today.

12/5/81

Today is my birthday. Woke up to a heavy snowstorm. Spent a couple of hours boarding up the fence in the barn so that the horses won't get out again. Split firewood for the next week. Cleaned up around the barn and house. The snow turned to rain just about the time I started to work on the cabin. Decided to put the thermostat back in my truck. As I was tightening up the last bolt, I broke one of the ears off the thermostat housing. Spent the rest of the day trying to patch it up so I could get to Kalispell. Put on the chains and went to

Polebridge to have supper with Karen and Bettie and Wilhelm. Karen had baked me a birthday pecan pie. Went to the saloon and played Busto until midnight. Had some boudain at the store and then back to Costello's. The weather was still warm at 1:00 a.m. and the snow had turned to slush. I could just barely get up Vance Hill even with chains. The car (truck) was running hot by the time I got to Costello's.

Sun 12/6/81

Took the broken piece off the truck and wired it together. Put it back on – it didn't seem to leak. Fed horses, went to Polebridge store, to Frank Evans' to get a piece of cake he had given me but that I had forgotten at his house. The North Fork had about 1 ½" of ice on it – very slippery. It would be impossible to drive it without chains. The truck stopped running before I got to Columbia Falls. The distributor was wet inside – probably from all the slush splashing on it. I wiped it out and dried it with matches, ran O.K. then. Washed clothes in Columbia Falls and then to Glacier International Airport to pick up Kathlyn Hurst at 8:34 p.m. She had a large ice chest full of seafood and other goodies that didn't arrive with her luggage. Stayed in Kalispell this night.

Mon 12/7/81

Had several errands to run in town today. Checked with the airport at 12:45 p.m. to see if the ice chest had come in on that flight. No luck! Since the next plane from the far south was to arrive at 8:34 p.m., we decided to wait until then. In the meantime, Frontier Airlines checked all possible routes and still couldn't locate the ice chest. We spent the day running errands and getting food and supplies. The ice chest didn't come in on the 8:34 flight. We were very disappointed now as the seafood would soon begin to spoil. Stayed in Kalispell again in the hopes that it might arrive tomorrow on the 12:45 p.m.

flight. Talked to Mom today. Having problems with the workman's comp claim and with someone molesting the people in the trailer park. Also talked to Helen – made arrangements for Lisa to visit me for Xmas. It doesn't look like Kevin will come. He won't be able to leave his work, doesn't have money etc.

Tues 12/8/81

Tried to call the insurance co. about Dad's workman's comp claim. The agent wasn't there. Ordered part for the truck and went to the airport to check on the ice chest. It still didn't come in. We couldn't wait any longer – we headed for the North Fork. The road was icy but not slushy. It was much better than on my way down, but still slippery. We put the chains on and used them all the way to camp. Stopped by the Polebridge store to bring Karen her bread etc., talked to her a while and went to Costello's. Stopped by the Dziuk's to tell them we will celebrate Johnna's birthday tomorrow. They had fed the horses today. And Joyce O'Hara had fed them yesterday – all is O.K. We went to Costello's to get the snowmobile and to go to the cabin. Kathlyn found it impressive. Took a ride down the North Fork on the snowmobile – There was slight snow flurry in the air.

Wed 12/9/81
To Polebridge store to call Helen, Mom and the insurance company. The insurance agent was sick and Mom wasn't home. Looked around the store, went to the pole bridge and took pictures of the river. And then to the Hostel, back to

Costello's to bake a cake and fix some hamburger steaks with smothered onions for supper. Brought the snowmobile to Dziuk's for them to ride. Today we celebrate Johnna's birthday. Had coke and wine. While the kids road the snowmobile we visited with Cheryl and John Dziuk. Took a ride to Spring Creek on the snowmobile with Kathlyn and then back to Costello's to eat.

Thurs 12/10/81

Last night the wind blew perhaps 60 M.P.H. The first time I've seen this kind of wind up here. The Dziuks later today, also said they hadn't seen this much wind since they have been here either. They have been here several years. Fed the horses, cats, did the daily chores and went to visit Frank Evans. Gave him a bottle of homemade strawberry wine. And got a link of his smoked summer sausage for a gumbo Friday night. Tasted his homemade crabapple, rhubarb, and elderberry wine. Also tasted his whole pickled pea pods and smoked summer sausage. Took pictures of his root cellar and cabins, and swimming pool (Ha!) Back to Costello's

to watch Chuck and Johnna while their mother went to the woman's social.

We rode the sled down the icy driveway. We also road the snowmobile around the horse pasture till dark. Kathlyn road the snowmobile for the first time alone today. Also her first sled ride. The road was so icy that the snowmobile just spun out. So, this is when we put it through the pasture – an excellent place to ride it. Started making the gumbo for tomorrow night.

Eagle photographer protests ticket

Editor's note: The following letter was written to U.S. Magistrate Jim Oleson. Due to its contents, the letter was not shortened and appears in its entirety here.

Dear H. James Oleson,

I am a photographer from Lafayette, La. I specialize in nature and put my photographs out for all the public to see. I have moved to Polebridge, Mt. in order to photograph nature here in Montana.

I had gone to McDonald Creek on several occasions to photograph the eagles there. In talking with one of the park service employees at the bridge, she told me that if I would come one morning (as this was the last time to take pictures), she would take me to a blind (researchers blind) only a couple hundred yards from the bridge.

On the 23rd of Nov. I came through the Park after picking up a friend who had flown in from Louisiana. I wanted to show him the eagles, and try for more pictures. We arrived in the middle of a snowstorm, and the weather was windy and cold. There was only one spectator on the bridge. I couldn't find any of the Park employees to take me to the blind.

I drove to the information center at Apgar only to find it closed. The sign on the door said it was closed due to the government's financial problems. Nowhere could we find anyone to show us to the blind. I didn't feel it would be a problem to anyone on a day like this to walk to the blind. When we got there, two girls were in the blind (researchers I assumed). They told me I couldn't stay, that there was a big fine for coming here, and that I should leave. I explained that I couldn't find anyone to take me here, and didn't know anyone was in the blind. I was nice to them, respected their work, and left quietly. They seemed nice also.

Then they pulled a sneaky one on us. Instead of concentrating on their research work, one of the girls ran down the path, and caught up with us. She walked along and talked nicely to us. The other one called the Park rangers — I assumed she was talking with them anyway, and it was convenient.

The girl walked very slowly, talked, and in general delayed us until the rangers got there. I was nice to the rangers also, explained that a Park service employee was to take me to the blind, but that I had made every effort to find one. I didn't wish to disturb anyone or anything, and in fact did not. Still, I was issued a $25 ticket which I had to pay on the spot with borrowed money. The whole situation was embarrassing to me, and I didn't wish to further embarrass my friend from Louisiana. I was very cooperative, as any of them will tell you.

I cannot go to Kalispell to dispute this ticket as I am working every day against the weather to get a roof on my cabin. It is a three hour round trip on icy roads from Polebridge and not financially feasible.

However, I wish to voice my extreme bitterness about the situation.

First, I do agree that I did the wrong thing and should have my hand slapped. But the $25 fine is not justifiable for walking a couple hundred yards down a path, a path I was to be taken down anyway. I did try to find someone, and did not use willful and wanton disregard for anything or anyone. I did not disturb the eagles (didn't even see one), the researchers, or the Park rangers. In fact, I feel they went out of their way just to "get" me. I was respectful and cooperative with all of them. I felt the ranger gave me the ticket because he was compelled to do so after being involved in their sneaky little caper.

In any case, I am put out by this, and feel that nothing has been accomplished by giving me their ticket. On the contrary, I feel now as many people here feel — that the researchers have taken a possessive attitude about the eagles and the area there. They should be willing to bend a little to accomodate the people who come to enjoy the eagles, just as the people must bend to make room for them. The Park is as much ours as it is theirs. I feel that under the circumstances, the ranger did not have to issue me a ticket.

I will always respect nature and its wildlife, as it is my love. However, I have no respect for this ranger, the Park service or the eagle researchers. They will not get my cooperation a second time — and besides, I don't like the sneaky and deceiving way it was handled.

James Hale
Polebridge

Fri. 12/11/81

Went to Polebridge store to call Mom, and to get mail. I had trouble getting through to Helen's office. In the meantime I worked on Bettie's car. There was a broken wire that was difficult to trace. I didn't have time to find it so I just ran one from the battery to the coil for now. Started the car and parked it in front of the store so she could get out of it (snowed a lot). I called insurance about Dad's claim. The agent (Mr. Swilley) with U.S.F. & G. seemed to be ready to settle for $20,000 lump sum. Called George Sobiesh – he didn't seem to think that was enough. He will help me check into it. I had written a letter to the U.S. Magistrate (Oleson) in Kalispell, and sent a copy of it to the Hungry Horse News. Today they published the full letter in the paper. Kathlyn had stayed at Costello's to finish the gumbo etc. I went back to get her, and to work on the cabin. I finished securing the rafters on the south east side. She helped me line them up. We went to Frank Evans' to

have a gumbo supper. Karen and Bettie came over also about 6:30 p.m.   John Frederick dropped in later and had a bowl of gumbo also. Frank's wine was beginning to affect Kathlyn. Took Karen and Bettie to the store and then went back to Costello's. Kathlyn had been staying at Costello's. He had 2 bedrooms and it was more convent for me not having to go to get her at Polebridge every day. Richard and Debby Hurst will be coming next month. We will probably be staying in Frank Evans' cabin by then. It doesn't have the modern facilities that this one does, but it does have running water.

Sat. 12/12/81
Went to Mc. Donald Creek to see the Eagles. The road was covered with ice and even with chains was slippery. Stopped along the way to take pictures. We saw only one eagle at the creek. Drove to Big Mountain to look over the ski area there. We couldn't ride down the lift so we didn't see the area from up above. This looks like a nice ski area. I will try to come back here and learn to ski. We had a nice supper at the Black Angus in Kalispell. Neither of us had eaten today, and was hungry. We stayed in Kalispell for the night. Yesterday the temp dropped to below 0 and there was not enough antifreeze to keep the truck radiator from freezing. I had lost a lot of it from the broken thermostat housing. Fortunately it didn't break anything, but the heater coil didn't thaw out until we got to McDonald Creek. It was cold inside the truck until then. Tonight I drained the water and put in 2 gallons of antifreeze.

Sun 12/13/81

Up at 5 a.m. and to the airport by 6:30 a.m. Kathlyn's plane had been rescheduled and left at 6:19 a.m. rather than 7:05 a.m. She made a Republic Airline plane leaving at 7:15 to Spokane. She could then transfer to Frontier, and still make her connecting flight in Denver. We were lucky. I drove to Columbia falls and washed my clothes. Then I stopped by Frank Evans house to take pictures of his place for him to take to take to New Zealand. To Costello's to feed horses, cats and to light the stove. Temperature last night dropped to -13° at Polebridge. Temp inside the house was 28 but the water pipes were just beginning to freeze. I worked on the cabin until dark. Went riding on the snowmobile and ate supper with Karen, Bettie, Ron Wilhelm and John Frederick

Photo of Frank's rental Cabin and Outhouse

Above Photo of Frank Evans' and his dog Pandora
Below Frank's cabin and tall swing on the left side of the Cabin

Jim standing to the left of Frank's swing

Mon. 12/14/81

Up at 7:30 a.m. Went to Columbia Falls with Frank Evans to get some lumber for his cabin. Drove to Kalispell to check on truck and part (not in), to get some pies, and for Frank to order another motor for his bicycle. Returned to Polebridge – around 2 p.m. Had some left over gumbo at his house and went to feed the horses and work on the cabin. Started the first board for decking the S.E side today. Weather was beautiful with 2" of new fallen snow. Cooked and wrote till after midnight. Thought a lot of my dad today.

P. S. As we were coming to an intersection in Columbia Falls, a car was turning in front of us. The door flew open and a boy about 8 years old fell out. His fall was cushioned by the snow and he rolled. He seemed O.K. – Looked like he was more scared than hurt.

Tues. 12/15/81

Woke up to a snow storm. Went to Polebridge to get mail and make phone calls. Helen said Lisa had decided at the last minute not to come to Montana. I was planning to leave tomorrow to pick her up in Calgary, Alberta Canada. I also talked to some insurance people about Dad's claim. It seems $20,000 lump sum is too low. $30,000 should be more in line. Called Mom – She is having trouble with someone knocking on trailers and rattling door knobs. Also talked to Kevin and David. Kevin wants to buy a jeep for $2,000. It's a '71 homemade job with oversize wheels and David thinks it is worth about $1,400. Made a sled for Karen to haul things around the place with. Went back to Costello's to feed the horses and cats. I picked Frank up with the gumbo & some apple dumplings he had made. Then I went to Polebridge store and we had supper with Karen & Bettie.

Letter from Lisa (Dated Dec. 10 1981)

Hi Dad, How's the weather up there? I bet it's nice. With all that snow and all. It's still pretty warm over here. It's trying to get cold. But it's not doing so good. It gets cold in the morning and hot in the afternoon. I wish it would hurry up and make up its mind. Sorry I didn't write to you sooner. But I try not to think of you because when I do, I start crying. Because I love you very much and I can't stop wishing you were here. But what's the use of trying anymore. I still miss you and as hard as I try, I still can't stop crying and wishing you were here. I can't wait to go up there and see you again. I need to tell you. When I seen you at the funeral home I was feeling bad until I seen you there and you made me feel so good. And I know that when I go up there. We will have a great time. Just being together again.

I guess Mama told you about Kevin. Dad I really don't know what's wrong with that boy. He had it made over here. But he just wanted more. Mama was trying to teach him responsibility. Kevin even said that Mama wasn't teaching him responsibility. And he goes and vandalizes Mama's car just because she won't buy him a car. Even if she wanted to she just don't have the money. And if she did. I would stop her before she did. Because that car would be demolished before he got 19. Because I rode in Mom's car before when he was driving. And one time we were going down the road over here and he turned the corner and the car went in circles and spun around. And we were facing the opposite direction. And one time we were going to the park and on the way. He kept going off the road and half-way in the ditch. Just to hit a box that was on the side of the road. And when the box was stuck underneath the truck he was going off the road and in the ditch to make the box break loose. And they had cars on that road too. This isn't the only things that he's done when he was driving. There's lots more. Like who would leave the keys in the truck when it broke down and you had to leave it on the side of the road. And the cop told Mama that she couldn't press charges on him for breaking her back window on her car. Because all of the jails were full and if he didn't have the money to bail himself out they would just let him go free. And he suggested Psychiatric help. So Mama was going to get him help and that's when he ran away and hitch hiked and went live with David and Alice. I guess he thinks that they are going to buy him a car. I don't see how he could do that to Mama. He hurt the best woman in the world. She may not show it but I know that she is hurting. I mean she has gone through a lot to put him through school and he quits when he is a senior. Just to go live with David and Alice. And they're not going to do any more than Mama would. And she has gone through a lot just to keep him healthy and alive. When he was sick she cared for him and when he needed help or a job; she got it for him but he just threw it all back in her face. It wasn't her fault that he couldn't hold a job his only problem is he is trying to rush himself too much. He wants to be out on his own so bad that he is not giving himself time to grow up and mature. Well I guess it's time to go. I need to get up and clean the house. So when Mama gets home she doesn't have to do it.

Love, Lots, Lisa
I miss you.

See You at Christmas

Wed 12/16/81

I woke up just before daylight and spent the early morning taking pictures of the beautiful sunrise. About an hour after sunrise it clouded up, and remained cloudy for the rest of the day. I went to Polebridge on the snowmobile and let Karen drive it around a little. We went to the frozen stream behind the Hostel & cleared off the snow where the skating rink was (just an area on the frozen stream where some of the local people had cleared it for ice skating). Then we went to the store and had a bowl of gumbo. Picked Frank Evans up around 1:30 p.m. on the snowmobile and he helped me finish the decking on N. W. side of the cabin. Then we went to his house and had some soup, venison and apple dumplings. Picked up Karen and Bettie, and we all went to see the movie "Cat Balou" at John O'Hara's house.

Thurs. 12/17/81

I wrote some letters for a while this morning. Then I fed the horses, cats etc. and went to work on the cabin. Decided to cover the decked side of the roof with tarpaper before the snows come again. It seems so simple, but yet is so difficult for one person to roll tarpaper on a 45° pitched roof. Quit about 3:00 p.m. to go Polebridge & call David. We talked about a half an hour or so about Kevin and the Jeep. Then I took Bettie for a short ride on the snowmobile. She spotted an animal in the woods. When we went over to investigate there were 3 moose in a bunch. We went back to the store to get

Karen and her camera. She took 3 pictures before they ran into the woods. Went back to camp and put on another layer of tarpaper before dark. Back to the store to have supper with Karen and Bettie. Went up a steep narrow trail and got the snow mobile in deep powder. Couldn't pull it downhill because the skis dug in. Couldn't pull it uphill – it was too steep. Couldn't move it to the side because of the cliff. Finally packed snow under the tracks & skis, enough to get a running start. Wrote Christmas letters (have no cards) until sometime after midnight.

Fri. 12/18/81

To Polebridge to get my mail and to call Mom. She is sick with a virus (influenza). Took my camera and trailed the moose we saw yesterday. They went haphazardly all over the place, often crossing their own path several times – they seem scatterbrain. After an hour or so of this I gave up and went to work on my cabin. Finished the tarpaper on the NW side, and put up a couple of rows of decking on the South east side before dark. Went to

Up the North Fork

by H. Frank Evans

Several from the North Fork were with the many who gathered in Whitefish last week for a surprise birthday party for Mary McFarland on her 80th birthday.

There has been mutual dismay among the neighbors at the treatment of Jim Hale for attempting to show the eagles in the Park to his friend from Louisiana. The matter might have at most deserved an admonition. The researchers sneakily delayed him which resulted in an arrest and fine. We thought it shameful and very harsh for a guy who wouldn't commit the crime of running a stop sign.

Now that the mountains blush pink at 4:30 p.m., we have scarcely more than eight hours of daylight. No wonder the cold runs deep. And strangely it is during our northern winter that the dear old earth is nearest to the generating sun. It is due to the wiggle of its axis as well as its elliptical voyage around sol that results in our season. Thanks for seasons!

Monday, the 21st, we again pass the solstice — though we celebrate it four days later. It is but an imaginary point in the infinity of time and endless void of space as we circumnavigate the sun in that annual 600,000,000 mile voyage at the breathless speed of 1,100 miles per minute...or so I'm told.

Man has been mesmerized by the solstice since long before the name Christmas was attached to the occasion. It harks back to our beginnings. It is vintage wine from an old bottle encased in cobwebs of ancient cultures.

Christmas is an anomoly of our rather sophisticated civilization. While originating with a celestial event, it has incorporated the cultural freight of myth, symbols, icons and song.

Celebrated as a day of selfish giving, we teach it to children as a day of acquisition or a day of gain and getting. Approaching Christmas, a child's optimism rivals that of a ski resort report. Letters of "I want..." go out to Santa by the millions but how many thank you letters does he get?

I, too, am joyed by Christmas and delight in green leaf and red berry, gay song, the pungency of pine boughs, greetings from friends, the creak of snow underfoot, the ringing of bells and cash registers, the solemn cry for peace, the sincere concern for the less fortunate, the rejoice of longer days to come though the nights shall grow colder and the snow deeper and the human problems more complex.

Merry Christmas, happy holidays, season's greetings, joy, peace, love, heaps of happiness and fun-filled days from us up here in the dark green woods and deep snow.

Polebridge to have supper with Karen, Bettie and Karen Reeves. We all went to Ron Wilhelm's for cake and homemade ice cream. The Hungry Horse News came out today. Three articles in it supported my letter published last week about the ticket I protested. Seems I stirred up a lot of reaction here. We need a little action anyway and these people need something to talk about. There were several people at the ice cream party – two of them were park service people. I'm sure they must have felt awkward as everyone was against the action of the Park Service on this matter.

Sat. 12/19/81

Today the weather warmed up to 32°. Instead of snow we had rain. I decided to do some inside things. I adjusted the track brakes, carburetor etc. on the snowmobile, split enough firewood to last a month. Later today the rain turned into a fine mist. I went to the cabin and worked on evening out the rafters for the decking. Worked maybe 1½ hours before dark. Took a bath, put on clean clothes for a change, and went to have dinner with Karen, Bettie & Ron Wilhelm. About 8:30 a.m. the group of 7th Day Adventist from up Moose Creek came by to sing Christmas Carols. There was about 20 of them. – They had an accordion, bells etc. The night was clear, full of stars, snow on the ground & they needed flashlights to read their music. It was like the kind of Christmas caroling you would read about in a storybook – very nice. I took Karen to the Hostel to check the stoves, feed cats, dogs etc. as John Frederick was on vacation.

Sunday 12/20/81

Finished evening out the rafters and decking about half the south east side before dark. The Mountains today were really pretty. The sky was clear except for a blue-black sky behind the snow white mountains. A few pure white clouds were over the mountains and the contrast against the dark sky was spectacular. Could see 30 miles or so into Candida. Went to Frank Evans' with Karen and Bettie for a spaghetti supper. I have run out of nails so Frank gave me a box to take to camp. Took Karen to check the Hostel & then went back to Costello's.

Old Cabin Near Vance Hill

Mon. 12/21/81

Called Mom about the workman's comp. claim. She was sick with the flu. Someone is still molesting her & the people in the trailer park at night. Finished decking the rest of the south east side except for 2 strips at the top that I must first rip. Trimmed the end of one side before dark. Went to Polebridge to pick up Karen and Bettie to go to Karen Chadwick's (goes by the name Karen Reeves). She is the wife of Douglas Chadwick who wrote for the National Geographic, but has maintained her maiden name. It seems several people do this here in Montana. Frank Evans was there also. We had an excellent Greek meal. Today was one of those cold days (about 5°) when the nails stick to your fingers, your hands stick to the aluminum ladder etc. I don't use the gloves on my left hand because I can't feel the nails with one on.

Old cabin near Vance Hill
(just North of Polebridge)

Tues. 12/22/81
Went to Frank's so he can show me what he wanted me to look after while he is gone. He plans on being gone for a week. He'll be back for a few days and

then will leave to spend a couple of months in New Zealand. He wants me to stay in his cabin and keep his dog "Pandora" company. I picked up the gloves he got for me and a couple for Bettie (Karen and her boyfriend Larry's Christmas gifts). As well as a pair of cross country skis for Karen (Bettie's Christmas gift). Went to the store to get mail and smuggle the gifts to Karen and Bettie. Fitted the decking at the top of the cabin and rounded it off on top

Wednesday 12/23/81
Waited till 11 a.m. for the weather to warm up a bit, I needed to lay tarpaper today, but in really cold weather it breaks or cracks instead of bending. Also, the heads of the tacks tend to break off more often. It warmed up to 3 and it was trying to snow. Decided to lay tarpaper before the roof got covered with snow, had the tarpaper in the house last night to warm it up. Also, borrowed Frank's torch to heat it where it needed to bend. I ran short on tarpaper. Had some pieces, but decided to go up to Red Meadow supply and get a roll. They didn't have any left, asked a couple of neighbors there, but they didn't have any either. Tried to get up the hill without chains, but began sliding backwards. Got my rear wheel in deep snow near the ditch and could neither go forward nor backwards. Jacked up one side to put the chains on. One of the Red Meadow people came by and helped me put the other one on. As I was trying to get up the hill, the right tire spun out on a rock and ripped the chains into pieces. At least I was on the road again. I backed down the hill for about a half mile. Went to Phil Sue's place where we rigged one of his old chains on my truck. With a little help of his 4 wheel drive I was able to get the truck back up the hill to the North Fork road. Gave him back his chain and went to Frank's to light his stove and feed Pandora. To the store for supper with Karen and Bettie. Karen had picked up the part I ordered for the truck. The wrong one in today; just isn't my day. Helped Tom Sluiter get his truck up his driveway. It took about one hour to go ¼ mile. An afterthought of yesterday as I was coming up Vance Hill a large truck carrying tanks was coming down. We met on a curve where the road was plowed too narrow for us to pass. He couldn't stop and we both went as wide as we could. I ended up in the snow bank on the side of the road. He stopped and helped me out. It's better I went into the snow rather than him. I had the mountain side – he had the cliff on his side. Saw 15 elk today.

Thursday 12/24/81

Fred horses and went to Polebridge store to call Mr. Hurst about final arrangements for Richard and Debbie to come here on the 3rd. Picked up mail and packages (mail came today since tomorrow is Christmas). Went by to check Frank's place, light fire etc. Went to cabin and put the short pieces of tarpaper I had left up on the roof. It began to snow heavily just as I was finishing – today I give myself a Christmas present– I am virtually finished with the roof. It's been a long hard lot of work and frustration, etc. to reach this major stage of construction. It's a good feeling to know I can get off that icy roof and work under cover in any kind of weather. Cut green truss, got the little pinecones "alarm clock" I had stashed under the wood pile to decorate the store for tomorrow's open house. Cooked rice and meatballs with mushroom soup to have dinner with Karen and Bettie. Helen called after dark from her office to wish me a Merry Christmas – she seemed lonesome. She connected me with David so I could talk to him, Mom, Dot, Jesus and wished them all a Merry Christmas.

Friday 12/25/81

Woke up at daylight – coyotes howling just below the bluff. Snow was falling, a beautiful Christmas day. Fed horses, cats etc. and went to cabin to put visqeen over the windows and door to try to close it up. Lit Coleman heater and stove to try to melt the ice on the inside logs. Went to Frank's to check things out there. Brought Pandora with me to the store (Pandora is Frank's dog), Karen, Bettie and I opened our presents together. They gave me a pair of snowmobile goggles. I felt bad I hadn't gotten anything for them. Karen Reeves gave me a jar of her homemade huckleberry jam. Helped them get ready for the open house. Took the truck back and picked up the snowmobile so I could ride the kids on it. Spent the afternoon at the open house. Most everyone left on the North Fork. Temperatures dropped by perhaps 30 or so. Had a Christmas turkey dinner with Karen, Bettie, the O'Haras and Karen Reeves. Called Pat to wish her a Merry Christmas. She had everyone over to see house for Christmas dinner. It was good to talk to her. And she seemed glad to hear from me. Took the snowmobile to Spring Creek to pick up a container of water and brought it to Rob Fisher. He couldn't carry it on cross-country skis – the snowmobile was the ideal way. Went for a midnight snowmobile ride in the trees and meadows below the bluff. Jumped a few hills for an hour or so before turning in. I had a nice Christmas.

Saturday 12/26/81

Couldn't sleep last night. Tom Sluiter woke me up around 10a.m. He had come to help me on the cabin. We watched deer in the meadow below, also saw a coyote. They were howling quite a bit today. Did the chores and then went to the cabin. We set up the stove under the cabin so as to try to generate enough heat to melt the ice. Rob Fisher came over to visit awhile about 3:30 p.m. I took Tom back home on the snowmobile and went to check Frank's and feed Pandora. The sink drain in the rental cabin had frozen. And the sink filled up to 1" before overflowing, before the tap froze. We were lucky – we could have had a room full of ice had the tap not frozen. Stopped by to say hello to Karen and Bettie. Went to Tom Sluiter's for supper. Took his son, Marcus, riding on the snowmobile. Saw another deer on the way to Tom's tonight. So many animas around now – such a change from the scarcities during hunting season. Went back to Costello's after supper to check fire and to get my pictures. Spent an hour or so looking at them with Tom and Genny.

Outhouse at old cabin near Vance Hill

Sunday 12/27/81

Spent the day doing chores and keeping the fires going at Costello's, Frank's and my cabin. Cleaned house and began gathering up my things to move out of Costello's. He is due back today. I will go stay at Frank's while he is gone.

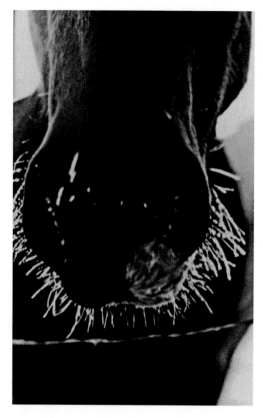

Monday 12/28/81

Fed horses and finished cleaning up the house. Went to check out Frank's place. Costello had called the store and he will be back tomorrow. Worked a couple of hours on leveling the floor joist. Put a nail in my mouth by mistake. Temp. was around 5 and it stuck to my lip. Without thinking I hurriedly took it out and pulled part of my lip off with it. I won't do this again. Had supper with Karen and Bettie. Spent the rest of the night writing letters (till 12:00 midnight). Have gotten a couple of small cuts and splinters on my hands from tamarack. This wood has something in it that aggravates the cut and keeps it from healing.

Tuesday 12/29/81

Fed horses, did chores and went to get mail. Tried to call Don Vinson about extending my leave of absence from 1/27/82 to 5/27/82. He wasn't in. Spent a couple of hours leveling the floor joist. The Costellos come in today. I have packed everything in the truck to move down to Frank's cabin. Left the snowmobile – Jerry will bring it down to me in the morning. Frank came in with his girlfriend, Ginny. Had supper with Karen, Bettie, 3 of Karen's girlfriends and the 2 Park Service people from the Polebridge station. Tonight I saw the northern lights for the first time. They looked like hundreds of spotlights shining up from over the horizon. They covered a large width of the horizon. They were clear and didn't have the color of some I have seen in pictures. Within 30 minutes, they were hidden by clouds. Slept at Frank's rental cabin. Had a hard time getting the fire started – it was cold – slept in my down sleeping bag.

The North Fork Hostel

Wednesday 12/30/81

Jerry Costello brought me the snowmobile around 10:30 a.m. Took him back home and visited with him awhile. Finished leveling the floor joist and started putting in the blocks around the perimeter of the floor to support the decking. Had supper with Karen, Bettie and her 3 friends. Stayed at Frank's rental cabin.

Thursday 12/31/81

Today is the last day of the year. It has been a versatile and trying year for me. Have had a lot of sadness and hard work this year. I have, however, grown internally from it all. I have felt that I have been living rather than just passing time. I have learned a greater appreciation for the natural things of my world. Have learned a new life – a different perspective. Have gained faith in humanity – people here are friendly and helpful. Nothing here has been dehumanizing to me. Had breakfast with Frank and Ginny. Went for a snowmobile ride – I like jumping hills. Helped Karen and her friends clear off the ice skating rink. Had soup at Frank's house. Ginny and I went to skate on the rink. Karen and her friends, John Frederick, Frank and fellow by the name of Chuck came and joined us. We skated until nearly dark. Baked some macarons at Frank's to take to the saloon tonight – they were a disappointment. Had supper with Karen, Bettie and one of Karen's girlfriends. Went to the Hostel to take a bath, then to the saloon where everyone was to meet for the New Year's celebration. We all (about 50 people) had a great time. People crawling around under tables and hanging

from the ceiling joist – a crazy party. We all picked up Bettie and were carrying her around over our heads. She grabbed onto a ceiling joist and climbed up, hanging by her feet and hands, she wouldn't come down. Amazing for a woman of 66 years old. I was also impressed today at Frank Evans' – he had just learned to skate on ice and was out skating with us today at 70 years old. Hope I can be that active when and if I reach their ages. Home to Frank's rental cabin around 4 or 5 o'clock a.m.

Looking out from Frank's house

Friday 1/1/82

Frank woke me up with a whistle about 8 a.m. He wakes me each morning when breakfast is ready by whistling out of his front door. His cabin is about 100 yards from where I stay. Had homemade huckleberry pancakes for breakfast. Went by the store to make plans for supper with Karen and Bettie. Found out Jerry De Santo (the Polebridge park ranger) didn't quite get his truck to the ranger station after the party. He slid on the curve just before the Polebridge and plowed into the snow bank. He was pretty well loaded like everyone else. He just left his truck there and walked across the bridge. Was on my way to work on the cabin when I met Jerry Costello on the road. He talked me into going ice skating with a bunch of the guys at a rink they made behind Ron Wilhelm's house. We ended up playing hockey for the afternoon. For a guy just learning to ice skate, I'm sure getting an initiation. Took several hard falls, should have some black and blue marks tomorrow. This is a wild and rough game. I think I would like this game more if I could just learn to skate better. Went to Frank's cabin to change, then to store to pick up Bettie and Karen's friend, Hannan to have supper at Jerry and Sally Costello's. There were about 20 people there – it was a feast. There are so few people here that everyone knows each other and do things together. So, whenever someone has a supper or something, everyone is invited. Stayed at Frank's rental cabin.

Saturday 1/2/82

Moved my clothes etc. into Frank's study. Loaded snowmobile into truck and went to store to see if Karen and Bettie needed anything in town. Mai came today. To Columbia Falls and Kalispell to get supplies and take snowmobile in for checkup. Stayed at Blue and White motel in Kalispell.

Sunday 1/3/82

Spent the day doing a little shopping at the few open stores. Wrote letters and generally tried to organize my plans. Helen called to wish me a happy new year – talked to Mom and Mac for an hour or more. Called airport to check on Richard and Debbie Hurst's flight. It's running an hour late – had weather in Denver. The plane came in a little after 10 p.m. Had supper and stayed at Blue and White Motel. Two of Richard and Debbie's suitcases didn't arrive on the flight. Several others didn't get their bags. This is getting to be a habit with this airline (Frontier).

Monday 1/4/82

Spent the morning getting supplies and taking care of business in town. Stopped by the airport to see if Richard's luggage had arrived on the midday flight – it had. It had been snowing quite a bit during last night and today. There was about 1½ feet of snow on the North Fork Road. One of my tire chains was broken so I had to drive without chains – we made it to Frank's cabin O.K. Saw several deer along the way. Frank had prepared a clam chowder supper with apple dumplings for desert. He had invited Karen and Bettie over. We stayed with Frank in his cabin.

Tuesday 1/5/82

I ordered the floor lumber for my cabin – I will need it soon and must give the lumber company 2 weeks' notice. Went to Polebridge store to show Richard and Debbie around and to get my mail. Went to the cabin and then to see if we could ride horses at Costello's – they weren't there. We fed the horses and went back to Frank's. Took Richard to the meadow at the end of Polebridge Lane and let him ride the snowmobile back to Frank's to get Debbie to ride. Richard and Debbie decided to take the

snowmobile by themselves. They came back sometime later covered with snow – they had had an accident. Evidently they were riding together, jumped a hill, and turned over. They found out it doesn't run very good upside down. Fortunately the only damage to body or machine was a broken windshield. Frank, Richard and I went out and cut up a tree for firewood. Got the truck stuck in the snow in the driveway. I had bought some chains and tonight made a set of tire chains for the truck. Also, repaired the broken set. Had steaks for supper.

Wednesday 1/6/82

Had huckleberry pancakes for breakfast. The temperature last night dropped to minus 32° F. This is the coldest weather I have ever been in. The truck wouldn't start – the oil was too thick & the cold had weakened the battery. I had my boat battery in the house, and boosted the other battery to start the truck. Went up the road and cut up another tree for firewood with Richard and Debbie.

Frank stayed in and packed for his trip to New Zealand. Came in, had hot dogs for lunch & then to Hostel to get some skates for ice skating. I couldn't find mine – possible that they are in Costello's truck. Went to Wilhelm's and started on his hockey rink. Tonight Richard, Debbie and I fixed a fried shrimp & vegetable dinner. Had Karen and Bettie over. After dinner Frank left to go on his trip to New Zealand.

Thursday 1/7/82

Spent the morning cleaning house. Made a mess cooking dinner last night. And also had a mess when Richard accidently bumped a shelf support &

243

knocked it loose. Everything over the stove fell into the french toast mix, and all over the stove & floor. Lots of things Frank has balanced delicately supported. Must walk around cautiously in his house. We went to the cabin and worked on the floor for the afternoon. Stopped by on the way out and visited the Dziuks awhile. Back to Frank's cabin to feed Pandora and put a log on the

fire. Frank Vitale came by for a while

and talked a half hour or so. We were driving out of the driveway to go have dinner with Karen and Bettie when we got stuck again. The snowplow had come down the North Fork Road and piled up snow at the end of the driveway. We plowed into it, but not quite hard enough to break through. We got out shortly though, as we had chains on now. Karen had fixed an elk roast dinner with champagne, vegetables and rhubarb pie.

Friday 1/8/82
Began getting things ready to leave to go to Big Mountain today. Put 2 kerosene lanterns in the root cellar to try to warm it up inside. Got cabin ready for the renter who was to arrive soon. We all took turns riding the snowmobile. It had snowed nearly 2 feet more yesterday and last night – it was powder. The snowmobile wouldn't get up on top of it unless we got up some speed. Most of the time it ran under the snow. All you could see was a head through the top of the snow. It looked weird. At moderate speed you could only see a spray of snow as the powder flew over the machine. The

driver couldn't see anything unless he stood up or got up more speed to get the snowmobile on top. In most places the snow was waist deep. It was fun, but we all got cold and covered with snow. The snowplow came by just as we were leaving. Got stuck again in the pile of snow at the end of the driveway. Got free shortly though and went to

Polebridge store to give Karen a key to Frank's house (she was to feed Pandora). And to bring the snowmobile to her. Picked up meat for Dziuks from their locker in Columbia Falls, order a snowmobile windshield, and picked up 20 cases of beer for Karen in Kalispell. The roads were mostly black ice and the truck kept swaying from side to side. Several cars in the ditch along the way. I got out to check the road and could hardly stand up on it. Drove on to Big Mountain and stayed in the lodge there. We rented our skis tonight so we wouldn't have to wait in line in the morning.

Saturday 1/9/82

Had breakfast and started skiing around 10:00 a.m. I was just learning to ski. Had been on skis only once before. I fell twice getting off the lift until I learned to stand rather than bend over. After that I did O.K. Only fell a couple of times after that at the ramp. Fell several times on the slopes. Debbie stayed with me most of the day, while Richard skied the more advance slopes. We skied until the lifts closed at 4:30 p.m. Had something to eat and got some night lift tickets. At Big Mountain they have lights on the Triple-three lift area, and light the slopes for night skiing. We skied until about 8:30 p.m. I feel I have learned the basics today. I can parallel turn with confidence, but need to work on my right turn. For this turn I use my left leg for support. It is the one that I had a cartilage removed from the knee several years ago. I didn't realize how much I favored my right leg. And must learn to use the left one on right turns. Today we skied most of 10½ hours. The boots have worn blisters on the sides of my feet. I didn't have a ski outfit. I wore wool but was wet and cold by day's end. We turned in our rental skis and drove to Kalispell. Had some snacks to eat along the way.

Sunday 1/10/82

Woke up at 4:30 a.m., had breakfast and took Richard and Debbie to the airport. Their plane left at 6:20 a.m. Went back to Blue and White Motel and slept till 10:30 a.m. Today my muscles in my left leg are stiff, also my right shoulder hurts – must have twisted it in a fall yesterday. Washed clothes, bought a few groceries and drove back up the North Fork. Took some pictures of deer along the way. Brought Karen her beer and the Dziuk's their meat. John Frederick came by just as I was pulling into Frank's place. He wanted me to help him get his snowmobile running. Worked on it until dark – it started snowing again. Had supper at Hostel with John, Rosalind, and Mike Ream.

Monday 1/11/82
Helped John Frederick get his snowmobile running. Spent half the day on this. The machine didn't have the power needed to blaze the trail to the border. I loaned him my snowmobile for this. Worked on getting a miss out of his Jeep for a while. Went to Frank's, shoveled out the end of the driveway where the snowplows piled up the snow, lit fires, fed Pandora, etc. It was getting late to start any major projects so I took the opportunity to change the thermostat housing on my truck and to install the thermostat. Cooked bread pudding for tomorrow night. Today I feel sad – something is wrong.

Tuesday 1/12/82
Washed dishes, cleaned house and began fixing dinner for tonight. Went to store to get my mail. Oops - dinner I was fixing is for tomorrow night (for Karen and Bettie). No problem though – the bread pudding will keep and the meatloaf is all ready – just need to put it in the oven about an hour before dinner. Read letters, opened packages, wrote a couple of letters and went to work on the cabin. Took Pandora with me today. Worked by lantern light for a couple hours after dark. Stopped by Dziuk's on the way home. Began some of the writing I had come up here to do.

Wednesday 1/13/82

Awakened by Kurt Jenkins who is renting one of Frank's cabins. He paid his rent and we talked awhile. He is working for the University of Idaho in a project to record the quantity of big game in the North Fork. Called Helen and talked to Mom awhile. Also, found out the dog teams that are to race will start from Hamilton, Montana on the 30th of this month. I will try to take pictures of this. Took Pandora and went to work on the cabin. Stopped by Dziuk's and learned there is a movie tonight at O'Hara's. It was a little after 5 p.m. and the movie started at 7 p.m. Hurried back to Frank's to get supper started. Got stuck in his driveway. If I keep getting stuck like this and shovel off snow each time, pretty soon I'll have it

cleared out. Bettie and Karen came over shortly after I got in. We had a nice dinner and got to the movie about 7:30 p.m. As usual it was late starting so we got there just before it started. Saw Stagecoach with John Wayne. John Frederick brought the snowmobile back tonight. Have been thinking about my Dad a lot lately – also about Pat.

Thursday 1/14/82

Spent most of the day taking pictures. The sun would come out every so often so I took advantage of it. Went skiing (cross country) with Karen and Bettie for an hour or so. Back to Frank's about dark to write letters for tomorrow's mail. Had supper at the store with Karen, Bettie, Jim Cummings and his lady friend. Called Pat to wish her a happy birthday.

Friday 1/15/82

Frank called at 12:30 a.m. He was in Hawaii, was leaving tomorrow for New Zealand. He didn't sound too impressed with Honolulu. Mail didn't get through today, heavy snowdrifts. Worked on the cabin, finished putting in the blocks to support the perimeter of the floor. Jerry Costello came by camp and barrowed the snowmobile to haul in Ray Browns things to his cabin. Worked until about an hour after dark. Temp. Dropped to minus 23, had supper with Karen and Bettie.

Saturday 1/16/82

Mail came through today. Worked on chiseling out a groove in a wall log to support the rear of the floor. Made meat loaf the other night and brought it over to the store for supper tonight. Went to the saloon for dart and ping-pong contests. Home to Frank's 2 a.m.

Sunday 1/17/82
Up late this morning. Cleaned house and went to Ron Wilhelm's to play hockey for a couple of hours. Helped Karen fill propane bottles. Took Renata Gaffey on the snowmobile to Costello's house for a little get together. Home around 11 p.m. It has been snowing steady for some time now without a thaw. The residents say there is more snow now than they have seen in about 7 years

Monday 1/18/82
Helped John Frederick take the head off his snowmobile engine- It has a blown head gasket. The sun came out for a short while- Took a few pictures around Polebridge. Had John O'Hara come over to plow Frank's driveway with his tractor. The tractor was to light and not enough power for snow plowing. Cost me 25.00 for his time & expense. And spent all afternoon shoveling snow by hand. Had supper with Karen & Bettie. Went to Renata's to visit and look at her art work (drawings).

Tuesday 1/19/82
Wrote letters for mailing today, made phone calls- my lumber for the floor is ready at Superior in Columbia Falls. Peggy Gensler came over to use Frank's phone. Helped John Frederick take the front axle off an old jeep. His differential went out on his & we must change the whole thing. Had to use the snowmobile to get it to the front of his place. The axle was to heavy and the snow too deep to handle by hand. Jerry Costello had bought some vodka for me and left it at Frank's front door. I made a gallon of Kahlua with it. Had a tasty fish loaf with Karen & Bettie. Wrote a poem till 2am

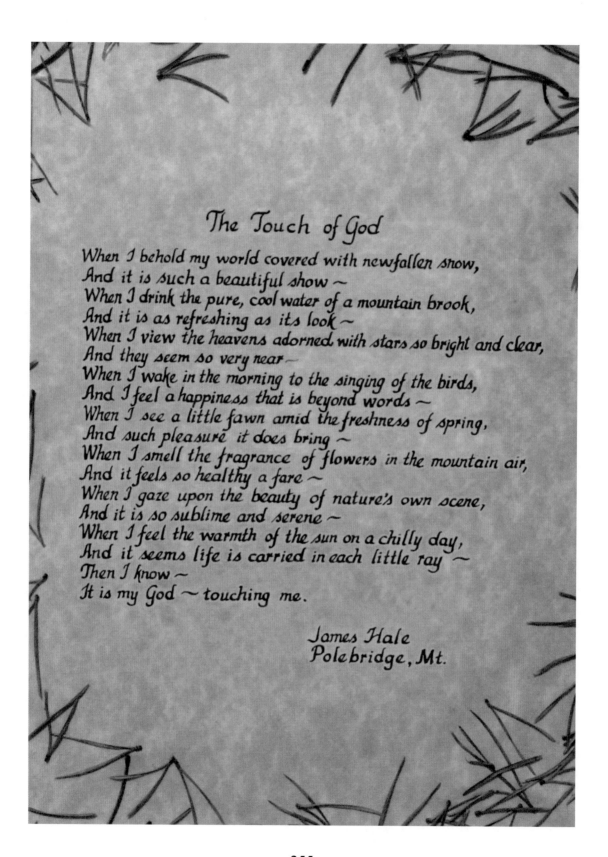

The Touch of God

When I behold my world covered with newfallen snow,
And it is such a beautiful show ~
When I drink the pure, cool water of a mountain brook,
And it is as refreshing as its look ~
When I view the heavens adorned with stars so bright and clear,
And they seem so very near ~
When I wake in the morning to the singing of the birds,
And I feel a happiness that is beyond words ~
When I see a little fawn amid the freshness of spring,
And such pleasure it does bring ~
When I smell the fragrance of flowers in the mountain air,
And it feels so healthy a fare ~
When I gaze upon the beauty of nature's own scene,
And it is so sublime and serene ~
When I feel the warmth of the sun on a chilly day,
And it seems life is carried in each little ray ~
Then I know ~
It is my God ~ touching me.

James Hale
Polebridge, Mt.

Wednesday 1/20/82

Up 7:30 a.m. to call Kathlyn Hurst about some business concerning the group insurance at the restaurant. Back to bed. Up again about 10:30 a.m. Went to John Fredrick's to change the front axle on his Jeep. It was cold and windy today. Too cold for working under cars. I lost my pocket knife somewhere in the snow around the jeep. To store for supper. Pierced Bettie's ears tonight-Karen has bought her some nice pearl earrings. Read and wrote till 1:30 a.m.

Thursday 1/21/82

Mom called to talk to me about Dad's debts. It was cold today (-2°) - got up to -20°F by 9 a.m. Decided to go to Columbia Falls to get my floor lumber rather than work on the cabin. Chill factor at Mariu's place was -105°F. The sun came out for a short while this morning. The cold had formed ice crystals in the snow and everything glowed with pretty sparkles. Wrote letters, read and worked on poem till 1:30 a.m.

Friday 1/22/82

To store for mail. To hostel to bring John Frederick a Jack I had bought for him. To cabin to unload lumber. I couldn't haul it in the driveway- snow to deep. Went back to get the snowmobile. Chuck Dziuk helped & we drug it in

Pandora

with the snowmobile. I jumped the berm with the snowmobile and buried it in the soft snow in the ditch. Took us half an hour to get it out. We decked half the subfloor before dark. Also ran out of lumber for this. Took a few pictures around the cabin. To John O'Hara's for his birthday celebration. Mac called and said the renter (Neil Martin) in New Iberia left without notifying him. The house seemed in a mess. Renata and her little girl Lilly came over to Frank's. We talked and looked at pictures till 3 a.m.

Saturday 1/23/82
To Renata's to bring back her X-Husband's dissertation she had loaned me to read. Took her and Lilly to the Hostel on the snowmobile. Came back to get Mike Reem and took him to the Hostel also. To cabin to chisel out the groove in the front log to support the floor. Also found a couple more boards and put them on the subfloor. To the store for supper. To saloon to elect a "non-official" Mayor. One contestant (Tom Ladenburg) didn't show so the speeches, election Etc. were postponed. Played charades till midnight.

Sunday 1/24/82

FWent to Ron Wilhelm's to play hockey. It had snowed about 1foot last night. And Ron had to use his front end loader to clear the rink. Played for about 3 hours. I made four goals today- getting better, this is a rough game. And some rough guys had several hard falls and collisions. One was a 3 way collision. After the game I had some ribs hurting on my left side. The sun came out for about half the morning. Temp warmed up to nearly 40° and caused the snow to form a crust on the top. Used the snowmobile to blaze a cross country ski trail down the loop road for Wilhelm. Snow was about 4 foot deep and I could only make 10 or 15 M.P.H wide open. Would get stuck if I stopped. Brought soup over to Karen's for supper. Then to cabin to cut out front door opening. Leveled log at door opening and moved the finish floor lumber inside. Supper with Karen and Bettie. To Corinne Spidel's to look over her drawings and help her with an idea for her book. To Frank's to cook bread pudding, pumpkin bread and make pina coladas. To bed about 1:30 a.m. The snow slid over the road at full hen hill today. No one can come in or go out until it is cleared. John Frederic found my pocket knife.

Monday 1/25/82
Mom called this morning to see if I had a copy of Dad's 1980 income tax. I did and will mail it to her. Tried several times after that to call out but something was wrong with the phone. Shoveled 1 foot of snow out of the driveway till 1 p.m.

Stopped by Costello's to arrange a gumbo supper, then went to work on the cabin till 7 p.m. Finished chiseling notch for lower floor and began leveling loft floor. To store for supper. Corinne and her friend John came over to Frank's to have Pina Coladas and look at pictures till midnight

Tuesday 1/26/82
Pandora woke me up at daylight with her wining. Kathlyn Hurst called this morning. Made several phone calls and then to store for mail. Spent the afternoon photographing deer between big creek and deep creek. This is their wintering grounds. Stopped by to see about getting more wood from Lee Downs- just missed him. Stopped and visited Ladenburg a while. To store for supper with Karen and Bettie.

Wednesday 1/27/82

To Lee Downs to see about getting lumber. It was buried in the snow behind his garage. And he wasn't too willing to dig it out. I visited an hour or so. And then spent the rest of the day photographing deer. I used the snowshoes for the first time today. Saw 30 to 35 deer. Saw a strange thing! Four deer were standing near the edge of the shore watching some ducks swimming in the river. One of the deer decided he wanted to stand on the other side of another deer. So he jumped right over the other deer's back rather than walking around him. Took about 35 pictures since yesterday. Missed a good shot of 3 elk walking across the river. Had supper with Karen and Bettie.

Thursday 1/28/82

My 6 months of absence was up yesterday. I haven't heard from Metropolitan about my request for an extension. I tried to call out several times this morning. But Helen's line was busy. Took the camera and went to see Bob Craft to ask if he had some 1X8 lumber. As I was driving down the North Fork just pass the road to my cabin a lynx crossed in front of me. I stopped to see if I could see where he went. He was just over the snow berm. He popped his head over and watched me from about 20 feet. I picked up the camera and got a shot of him. He walked around a little and crossed in front of me again. He was the biggest Lynx I have ever seen- maybe 35 pounds or so. I followed him for 100 yards or so, but the snow was too deep. Just as I was driving away another one crossed the road, then another and another- four in all. All of them were fully grown but not near the size of the first one. I went to Frank

260

Vitale's house and visited a while. He showed me how to get to Bob Craft's. Bob wasn't around but it seemed he was only running his stud mill. I went back to Frank's got the snowmobile and snowshoes. I tracked the four cats all afternoon (backtracked). I was hoping I could find their den. No luck. They seem to be hunting in a pack like wolves. They fanned out in the woods just in sight of each other. Sometimes even walking next to each other or even on the same trail, as one would walk around a bush looking for rabbits, the other walked around the other side. I found where they had killed a snowshoe rabbit, and ate everything but the skin. I felt lucky to see four lynxes together today. Also learned something today- lynxes are not always lone hunters- they do sometimes hunt in packs. Stopped by the Dziuk's today for a while to let the kids ride the snowmobile. Brought oysters over to the store and cooked fried oysters for supper. Went to Hostel to see Mike Reem. I took him to his tent. We pulled his toboggan sled in with a load of gear. Used the snowmobile. I borrowed a couple of predator calls from him. I will try to call in the cats. Home to Frank's about 1:00 a.m.

Friday 1/29/82

The Dziuk kids came over to Frank's and had biscuits while I ate breakfast. Went to store for mail. Drove the Dziuk's (2 of them) to their house on the snowmobile. And then to Red Meadow Road to see if Red Meadow Supply had any 1X8 lumber. Drove up Red Meadow road for 7 or 8 miles. Saw only rabbit tracks. It seems barren of game in the whole drainage. Back to Frank's to make phone calls. John Frederick came by and wanted me to help him work on his snowmobile. The water in Frank's cabin is running slower each day. I wanted to check it out first. We dug up the lines and all seemed O.K. The valves were fully open. The stream must just be freezing up. Worked on the snowmobile till 7:30 p.m. Finally got it running O.K. Went to store for supper with Karen & Bettie.

Saturday 1/30/82

Spent most of the morning cleaning house. Went to Camas Creek to take pictures of deer. Stopped by Lee Down's place to see about getting some lumber from him. There were about 10 deer in the trees near his house. I took a few pictures and then the sun went behind a cloud. Decided to dig out the lumber from under the snow while waiting for the sun to come out. It took a couple of hours to get enough lumber in the truck. The sun didn't come out again. Visited a while and then took the lumber to the cabin. Unloaded it at the end of the driveway. Went back for the snowmobile and drug it to the cabin. Two of the Dziuk kids helped. Had Oyster soup with Karen and Bettie. Changed oil in truck. Left snowmobile with Karen so she could use it to come to Frank's to feed Pandora and keep the fire going. I am going to Lost Horse Village for a few days to photograph the dog team race there. Today I ran the snowmobile to 70 M.P.H. Still don't know what top end is. I need more room. The North Fork Road is too curvy and rough for any higher speed.

Sunday 1/31/82

Heard on the truck radio that the dog teams had already started racing. Must have gotten my dates mixed up. Will try to find them in-route. To store to give Karen Frank's key & to cash a check. I was heading down the North Fork Road when I met Jerry Costello's friend "Heavy" coming up the road. He was coming around a curve downhill as I was approaching the curve. When we got in view of each other we both tried to pull to the right. I saw his truck going into a slide. I was on the outside of the curve hugging an 8' snow berm. We were on paths for a head on collision. I had no choice but to try to either plow into the berm or jump over it. I turned hard to the berm and just as I hit it, he hit me just behind the door. This turned my truck parallel to the berm so as I hit it, I only plowed snow along the edge of it. There was 8" of

new snow (wet and slushy) and it was still snowing heavily. He said he had hit his breaks to slow him. But that instead is what started his skid. He had extensive damage to his left front and left door. My left rear quarter panel was demolished. We were lucky not to have met head on- neither of us were hurt. We went to Lee Down's to have him come out & make a report. It is the second time I was hit up here on the North Fork. In one sense it seems unreasonable for a place so remote and with so little traffic. In another sense however, the people here drive too fast. There is always someone skidding into the railings or running off the road. Frequently I see where cars have plowed into the berms on each side of the road. If it wasn't for them, more people would go over the cliffs. One lady earlier this year lost control & was killed when she hit a logging truck. I also had to take the berm on Vance Hill to avoid hitting a large truck carrying tanks. He was coming down the hill too fast. And there was no room for both of us to pass. I must be as defensive as possible here. Now my truck really looks like a North Fork truck. Stopped by Columbia Falls Police Department, and made a report. Drove on to Hamilton Mt. only to learn the dog teams were now at the anaconda check point. The road from Hamilton to Anaconda was closed. It took me another 3 hours to go back to Missoula and around to Anaconda. I got there at 11 p.m. I learned the people with the dog teams were staying at the Trade Winds Motel. Some of them were still up. I spoke to them a few minutes. Loaned them my clock. I will go with them to the starting point in the morning

Monday 2/1/82
Up 6:30 a.m. Went to the café across the street, and talked with the guys with the dog teams. Spent the day taking pictures of the dogs & the race. The dogs are smaller than I expected. Most are Siberian huskies. Many are mixed breed. They tell me the big huskies are for pulling heavy loads. These

are bred for speed and endurance. They are pretty dogs, especially hooked up in the team. One of them tried to go around a lead snowmobile that had stalled. The whole team and slay fell down an embankment. They lost about 4 minutes trying to untangle the dogs, and get them up the hill again. The leg of the race was short today- just over 20 miles. Tomorrow they race 50 or 60 miles. The whole race is over 500 miles, and will last until 2/7/82. It's the biggest slay dog race in the lower 48 states. Seven teams are running. One from British Columbia, others from the US. The guys are as crazy as the dogs. Today they decided to go to downtown deer lodge, Mt. and feed their dogs on Main Street. Over 100 howling and barking dogs made quite a spectacle. The

dogs are tied to the vehicles with short chains. Had trouble putting gas in the truck today. Had to push the fender out with the hydraulic jack so it would clear the kinked gas line. My left side is still hurting today. May have cracked a rib in the last hockey game. Drove to Avon Montana so I would be near the next starting point in the morning.

Tuesday 2/2/82

Went down little Blackfoot river road about 8 a.m. The dog teams were there. I took pictures and helped with the dogs. It was snowing heavily with strong winds. Because of near blizzard conditions the track was shortened to about 45 miles. I left the teams and drove to the National Bison Range North of Missoula. The winds and snow were so heavy that visibility at times was no more than 50 yards. The flowing snow was like a "white out" and at times it was difficult to tell where the road was. I heard on the radio that the roads just behind me were closing. I was getting through just in time. Most of the roads in the Bison Range were closed, but I did get a few pictures of Elk and Buffalo. I used the predator call to draw (elk) their attention. This also drew attention of two other elk who were out of sight over the hill. They came in to

investigate. I drove on in to Kalispell and checked into the Blue and White Motel. I noticed the truck that had hit me parked at the motel. I knocked on the door and found Jerry Costello, Ray Brown "Heavy" and Joe there. They were waiting on Bill and Jane Brown. I joined

268

them and we all went to have pizza. All the guys had been trying to make Heavy feel better about the accident by telling him how bad that curve is and how many accidents occur there. He began thinking the accident wasn't entirely his fault and approached me about this. He wants me to say that "it was just one of those things". That we met on a one lane road and the accident was unavoidable. He wants his insurance to pay for his truck. And my insurance to pay for mine. I would like to keep the peace here because he is a friend of Costello's. But for me to say this would put an undue burden on my insurance premiums. I cannot deny that he was in an uncontrollable skid. And that he hit me on my side of the road. Besides Lee Downs investigated the accident and knows this also. It is also obvious that it is not a one lane road. There was plenty of room for us to pass in safety. I don't like this. He put me in a bind on the road- now he is putting me in a bind with our mutual friends. I'll try to reach a mutual understanding with him, but then I'll stand my ground.

Photo by: James W. Hale

Wednesday 2/3/82

Talked to "Heavy" (Robert Levy) today- let him know where I stand. To B & B to wash cloths and buy some groceries. To camera shop to get a cable release. To court house to check out taxes. To Kalispell Body shop for an estimate. Other errands. To Columbia Falls to get my loft floor lumber. Picked up Jerry Desanto's lumber. Took lumber to camp. Unloaded it at end of driveway. To ranger station to bring Jerry his lumber. Took Rich Upton to his house- visited a few minutes. To frank's to unload truck. The night is clear and beautiful. It is so bright, even with ½ moon that strong shadows are cast. Temperature is -20° by 9 p.m. last night was around -30. Tonight should be colder. The temperature drops so fast and so low that the trees in the surrounding woods can be heard to pop and crack from freezing. Sounds like small rifle fire.

Thursday 2/4/82

Temp at 8:30 a.m. – minus 39°. This is now the coldest weather I've been in. Spent the morning trying to take pictures of the birds at Frank's feeder, baking ginger bread, and general indoor chores. The sun was out. The sky was clear. And it was a beautiful day. Went to get my mail. To the cabin to move the lumber into camp. The Dziuk (Roxanne & Chuck) and John Frederick came over to help. We laid some decking before dark. To store for supper with Karen and Bettie. The moon was out bright tonight with a large distinct ring around it. The sky is beginning to cloud up. Shouldn't be as cold tonight.

Friday 2/5/82
The weather fooled me. It cleared up. Temperature dropped to -32°F. Had a long conversation with Mom this morning. Went to get mail. Went to Tom Ladenburg's land to take pictures of elk. The sun was out- it was a pretty day, but cold. I used snowshoes to get to the river. Covered myself and camera with sheets. Used predator calls to try to bring something in- no luck. Couldn't sit for more than an hour or so- I would get too cold. There is a pretty stream back near the river. Had only the telephoto lens. I will come back and take pictures of it. Saw a few deer but no elk. Stopped by Ladenburg's to invite them to supper tomorrow. To Dziuk's for supper. To Frank's about 10 p.m. – started fixing gumbo. Peeled shrimp till 3:10 A.M.

272

Saturday 2/6/82

Up late. Spent the day cooking and cleaning house. Had the Ladenburg's, the Dziuk's, Karen & Bettie over for supper – 13 in all. Everything turned out nice. Everyone seemed to enjoy the gumbo. Cleaned up after everyone left. Wrote and read till 1:30 A.M.

Sunday 2/7/82
Up at sunrise – a beautiful sunny day. Went to store to return bowls I had borrowed. To Ladenburg's to return a short story Joan Ladenburg had left for me to read. Went back on their land to take pictures of that pretty little stream and some deer. Set up a blind and waited most of the afternoon for something to show – no luck. It began to get cold by sundown, so I went back to the

truck. The break light switch on the truck had been malfunctioning lately and the brake lights were on. The truck did start however. On the way back I began thinking what would have happened if I had been closer to the berm when the accident happened. I drove closer to it and was sucked in. It stopped the truck so fast it threw my camera on the floor. Doesn't seem to be damaged though. I spent a half hour or so digging the truck out. A fellow stopped by and helped another half hour. We were making progress, but still couldn't get it out. Another fellow in a 4X4 loaded with firewood came by. He pulled me out with ease. To store for supper with Karen and Bettie. Fixed the starter rope on her generator. Back to Frank's about 10:00 p.m.

Monday 2/8/82
To Jerry Costello's to ask him over for gumbo tomorrow night. He, his friend Joe, and I drove down the North Fork Road to take pictures of deer. As we were stopped watching some deer, a moose came walking up the road. He was slowly coming to the truck. Then along came a logging truck and scared him 2 miles down the road. We followed the truck and caught up with him just off the road. Took a couple pictures of him. Took several deer pictures. It was a beautiful sunny day. Came back to the cabin and worked on the floor for about an hour before dark. Went to Costello's for supper. We all went to Ron Wilhelm's and played hockey by moonlight. The moon was so bright we didn't need lights to play by. Quit around 11 p.m. Karen, Bettie & Windy came over just when we quit and we played games with paper bags over everybody's head. Home to Frank's about 1:00 A.M.

276

Tuesday 2/9/82

Kathlyn Hurst called today – She plans to come to Big Mountain on the 21st. Called Helen – her Godmother (Aunt Sweet) died. And she was just leaving for the funeral. Talked to Mom – got cut off and couldn't get back through. Wrote several letters and got to the post office (Polebridge Store) about 2:00 p.m. Pandora road with me on the snowmobile. She has been riding hesitantly with me on short drives. But today she was eager to ride – jumped up on the machine without any coaxing. Took the Dziuk's (Cheryl & Chuck) to their house via snowmobile. To Costello's to get my camera I had left there. Took a couple of pictures of the cabin from the hill in front of it. The snow was waist deep (I sunk waist deep) and I had difficulty getting up the hill. Back to Frank's to fix gumbo & straighten up a little. Had 14 people over about dark. Had shrimp gumbo, beer, wine, pina coladas, kahlua, dips, coke. We all had a good time – everyone left about 10:30 p.m. Karen had sprained her foot skating last night and had to be carried in. Temperature last night dropped to -35 F. Would like to see temperature break the -40° F mark then winter can be over with.

Wednesday 2/10/82

Mom called this morning. I also had several calls to make about Dad's business. Cleaned the place up and washed dishes from last night's gumbo. To store to bring back bowls I had borrowed, To Costello's to bring a quart of gumbo for "Heavy", and to look for my lens brush I had lost. Worked on the cabin. Finished the subfloor. Also did a little work on the loft and the door. Took the gumbo stock over to the store and made onion soup with it. Wrote until about midnight.

Thursday 2/11/82

Spent the morning on the phone. Worked on the cabin until 3:00 p.m. Back to frank's to call Mac, and to make other business calls till 6:00 p.m. Seems Mac will have the house in New Iberia rented Saturday. Will have to sign a letter for the city stating that I will tear down the damaged part of the house by a given date, (probably 7/31/82).

Friday 2/12/82 Went to store for mail. Took Cheryl Dziuk back to her house on the snowmobile and worked on the cabin. Leveled two loft logs. Dug my collapsed tent out from beneath 4 foot of snow. Set it

up inside the cabin. Some of the poles were broken, and several were bent. But the tent seems O.K. To store for onion soup with Karen and Bettie. This is the end of the Gumbo. Went to Costello's to deliver a message to Joe & Heavy. Took a snowmobile ride in the meadow off the loop road. Read until 1 A.M.

Saturday 2/13/82
Temperature has warmed up today, snowing heavily – a wet snow. I'm concerned about the snow on Frank's roof. It has built up to nearly 4 feet now. Don't know how much weight this cabin can stand. Wet snow or rain will add a lot of weight. If it doesn't slide soon, I'll have to do something about it. Worked on the cabin all day. Finished leveling the loft and started cutting the groove in the front wall for the flooring to fit into. Went to the store to have supper with Karen & Bettie.

Sunday 2/14/82

Today is Valentine's Day. For the first time this winter we are getting a thaw. Temperature was warmed up to just above 32°F and it is raining. John Dziuk came by with Ladenburg's caterpillar and plowed out the driveway for me. Tapped on the roof from the attic with a timber trying to get the 4 feet of snow on the roof to slide. The rain is adding a lot of weight. Finally got about half of it to slide. Hope the rest slides sometime today. Took Pandora on the snowmobile and went to work on the cabin. Finished cutting the notch along the front wall to support the loft floor. Began fitting the first board along the wall for the decking. To store to have supper with Karen, Bettie & Ron Wilhelm. The road is slush over Ice. The snowmobile did a lot of sliding coming down Vance Hill. Went to Frank's to call Pat. Had to climb over 6' of snow to get to the front door. The rest of the roof must have slid. Called Pat until 1:00 a.m. her time. She wasn't in.

Monday 2/15/82

A rainy wet day. Took Pandora on the snowmobile (She goes everywhere with me now) to see if Costello had any 10D common nails – He didn't. Left Pandora there and went to Red Meadow Supply for a box of nails. Came back for Pandora and worked on loft floor all day. Chuck, Roxanne & Johnna helped. Finished all but the last board along the wall. John & Cheryl Dziuk came by just before dark. Went to the store for supper with Karen & Bettie.

Tuesday 2/16/82

Went to get mail – didn't get here till 11 a.m. Pandora and I went to the cabin via snowmobile. Fitted the last board along the wall. Fitted and set the two support logs from the purling strips to the loft floor. Cut the ends even on the loft floor. Worked on cutting the notches on each side of the door to insert 2X4s into. This is slow - will take some time. To store for supper with Karen, Bettie, Ron and Dianne Wilhelm and John Frederick. To Frank's about 10:30 p.m. Studied my pictures until midnight near the river most of the afternoon. Checked the bone pile I had set out. A small animal, perhaps a pine martin, had been around. The Dziuk kids took turns on the snowmobile. Cheryl Dziuk came by to get Chuck and Johnna for supper. All of us, including Pandora rode the snowmobile to their house. Had supper with Karen and Bettie. Went to John O'Hara's to see a movie.

Wednesday2/17/82

Took the snowmobile to the Hostel since John Frederic had some of my tools there. Spent the morning adjusting it, greasing it, straightening one of the wear bars, and giving it a general checkup. Went to the cabin and worked on chiseling out the slots on either side of the door. Johnna & Chuck came by and spent the afternoon with me. We watched elk feed

Thursday 2/18/82

Talked to Helen and Mom today. Stopped by store to bring tomatoes for tonight's supper. Have to use the truck today since the road is thawed in places & the snowmobile would have to run over gravel. Worked on cutting the slots on either side of the door. This is going slow. Set up tent on loft and moved floor lumber inside cabin. Went to store to have spaghetti with Karen, Bettie, Jerry De Santo and his son from Trail Creek.

Friday 2/19/82

Cleaned house a little. Shoveled snow off porch roof – the weight had broken a couple of rafters on the overhang. Peggy Gensler came over and used the phone an hour or so. I used Frank's pedal stone to sharpen my axe and two chisels. Spent 2 or 3 hours trying to locate the end of Frank's water line upstream from his house. Finally found it – The end of the line had a stopped up screen on it. Had to reach a couple feet under the water to work on

replacing the screen boxes. After less than a minute my hands and arms were stinging and a bit numb from the cold water. I can see how someone who falls in such icy water won't last more than 5 minutes. Went to store for mail, then to the cabin to work on the notches. Finished them by lantern light. Stopped by Costello's and Dziuk's to see if they needed anything in town. To store to have supper with Karen and Bettie. Karen was in town to get her foot x-Rayed. She returned about 9:30 p.m. with a cast on it. She had broken her ankle on ice skates about a week ago. To Frank's to feed Pandora, clean house, and get ready to go to Kalispell tomorrow.

Saturday 2/20/82
To the Hostel to arrange for John Frederick to feed Pandora and watch over his place (Frank's). To Columbia Falls & Kalispell to get food supplies etc. Met Sally Costello, Corrine Spiedel, Joyce O'Hara & Jane Brown at the Narge Washeteria in Kalispell. We all had a Rum and coke and went to a movie (In Golden Pond). After the movie we went to a place called 4-Corners. We danced, played pool and cut up till 2 a.m. Had breakfast at Perkins and went our separate ways about 3:30 a.m. We all had a good time piling in the cab of Janes truck, dancing etc. It was a change from the life on the North Fork. I got to know these girls better & enjoyed their company.

284

Sunday 2/21/82

Worked on fixing the taillights and a broken headlight on the truck. Adjusted the clutch. Went to meet the girls I was out with last night, and "Heavy" at the Stud Service Horse Auction. There were some nice stallions there. A funny thing happened – Some guy bid $200.00 and got the bid. He thought he had bought the horse. They had to explain to him that he bought a stud service and not a $30,000.00 horse. But he didn't have another horse to mate. They had to re-auction the stud service for that horse. Went back to the Motel later this afternoon and watched a movie on TV. Went to the store for a couple of things and then to Bill Brown's house. He helped me bleed the truck breaks. The girls came home and fixed pizza for supper. Left to go pick up Kathlyn Hurst at the Glacier International Airport. Her plane was about ½ hour late – arrived about 9:10 p.m. stayed in Kalispell.

Monday 2/22/82

Spent most of the days getting supplies I couldn't get on Saturday. Getting an estimate for the truck damage. Bringing the suitcases full of seafood to the locker, etc. Drove to Whitefish where we went to an interesting Taxidermy shop (Costello's Taxidermy). It was like a museum – had a lot of deer, elk, caribou that had unnatural and deformed antlers. Drove on to Big Mountain where we stayed at the Alpinglo Inn.

Tuesday 2/23/82

The weather had cooled off a bit and it snowed on and off most of the day. Began skiing about 10:30 and skied until the lifts closed at 4:30 p.m. At times the snow was so heavy we couldn't see if we skied very fast. Then at other times the sun was trying to come out and it was nice. Today I concentrated on improving my right turns, and have more confidence now. I think I'm ready for a more difficult slope. I traded my rented skis in for longer ones. Will try them tomorrow. By dark the sky was clear. It was turning colder. Had a nice dinner at the big mountain lodge.

Wednesday 2/24/82

Today we skied a couple of runs on the green slope at triple-three lift. Then we went to the mid-two lift, and skied one of the blue slopes there. Then we went to the top on the big-one. This is really a long one – 6,564 feet of lift run and 1,953 feet of rise. It was really pretty up on top with the trees so heavy with snow & ice that some of them bent over till the treetop touched the ground. It was really foggy though, and cold. Could see only a couple hundred yards. When we got down (blue slopes) Kathlyn's

feet and knee were hurting her. She did really good I thought, as some of the slopes were fairly steep and ice packed. I continued to ski on the mid-two lift. There were several blue slopes from this one. I met a guy from Saskatchewan Ca. who gave me a little instruction on turning. I practiced this until the lifts closed at 4:30 p.m. It seemed to really help me with control. I was even able to ski a black slope by days end. We took a break for an hour or two, then went night skiing on Triple-Three lift till 10:00 p.m. The weather was nice most of the day – snowed occasionally.

Thursday
2/25/82
A pretty day –
Took a few
pictures at Big
Mountain.
Kathlyn wanted
to check out
some of the
condominiums in
case they decided
to come to Big
Mountain to ski
this Christmas.

The ones near the ski area were nice, but none of them had TV's – A problem
for some of their group. To Kalispell to get suitcase full of seafood out of
freezer locker, buy groceries, get supplies for Polebridge store, Dziuk's meat,
coyote bones, etc. Saw several deer on the way up the North Fork. When we
got to Frank's my snowmobile was gone. Perhaps someone borrowed it, but if
not, I was worried. To store to get key & to drop off Karen's supplies. To
Dziuk's to bring their meat and to show Kathlyn the cabin. When we got back
to Frank's, we found a note on the door – John Frederick had borrowed the

snowmobile to invite
the girls at the
boarder to Karen's
surprise birthday
party tomorrow. I
was relieved to know
where it was. Had
crawfish stew for
supper. Began fixing
a dip for tomorrow's
party. Mac and Pat
both called tonight.
Saw the northern
lights tonight.

Friday 2/26/82

Chopped firewood. Kathlyn began making crawfish etouffee. John Frederick brought the snowmobile back. Gassed it up and filled the oil. Also filled chain case with oil & sealed drain plug. Took Kathlyn for a ride down the loop road and up the trail over Vance Hill. Went to check on the coyote bones and take pictures at cabin. Costello and his dog, Montana, stopped by. Went to Frank's to prepare the dip for tonight and to put up the crawfish etouffee. Went to the Hostel at 6:30 for Karen's surprise birthday party. Most everyone in the North Fork was there – it was a great party.

Saturday 2/27/82

Went to visit Karen and Bettie & to bring Karen a couple of birthday presents we had bought for her. Took a ride up the North Fork to the end of the plowed road – about 5 miles from the boarder. Back to Frank's to get suitcases. Drove on to Kalispell. Saw several deer (25 or 30) on the way down the North Fork. Also saw elk. Had a nice dinner at 1st Avenue west of Kalispell.

Sunday 2/28/82
Took Kathlyn to the airport to catch her 6:19 a.m. flight back to New Orleans, La. Drove to Columbia Falls. The gas stations weren't open yet so I parked at the Night Owl Café and slept in the truck for an hour or so. Tanked up the truck, got a few groceries and headed up the North Fork. Stopped to walk around & look for deer antlers for ½ hour or so. Spent most of the day installing the stove in the cabin. Finished just before dark. John Dziuk had come by, and helped me at the end. Went to the store to have supper with Karen, Bettie and Ron Wilhelm.

Monday 3/1/82
Took Pandora with me to go work on the cabin.

Photo of driveway leading to the cabin

Lit a fire in the stove for the first time. Don't know how this stove will do. It smokes when it is opened to add wood. Does fine otherwise. Worked all day on making the door jam, Chuck and Johnna came over for a while. Ron Wilhelm stopped *Photo of driveway leading to the cabin* by also. It snowed most all day – about 8" of snow on the ground. Took Karen and Bettie some crawfish stew and stuffed bell pepper for supper.

Tuesday 3/2/82
Finished writing letters, and went to get my mail. The weather was unusual today – a low fog hanging just above the ground. Took Johnna and chuck back to their house. Put more bones out for the coyotes. Went back to get Pandora and went to work on Cabin. Finished the door frame, and started on the picture window. Had dinner (supper) with Karen & Bettie. Today two bald eagles flew up and perched on the dead Tamarack snag in front of the cabin. They stayed there 20 minutes or so. Frank Evans called about 10:30 from New Zealand. His flight back to the states will arrive on 2/12/82. He plans on visiting his girlfriend Ginny in Colorado before returning home.

Wednesday 3/3/82
Took Pandora and went to work on the Cabin. More snow last night makes riding the snowmobile easier. The frozen slush was like riding on the cement. Spent the day casing the picture window. Finished about dark. Ripped molding for the glass by lantern light. It snowed heavily at times today.

RINGO

They all knew him by his trade,
This man no one would evade.

He hails from the deep South, they say,
And to the North he made his way.

He was easily recognized in the dead of night,
For he wore a mustache of white.

Under government contract he did his business,
Covering the North Fork with all its wilderness.

Through dust, mud, or snow, he would venture,
To carry out his job in any temperature.

He worked his four plus four,
With all the power of its bore.

And when his job was done,
He would return only to prepare for another run.

Ben Ringo was his name,
The U.S. mail was his game.

James Hale
Lafayette, Louisiana

Thursday 3/4/82

Installed the glass in the picture window and the door is covered with visqueen, the stove can really heat the place. Had to cool off outside every once in a while. Need the heat though to dry out the loft floor so I can seal it. Swinging the axe on the window cutout has got my right shoulder hurting again. Only one more window though, and I can relieve it by working on something else.

Friday 3/5/82

To get mail at 10 a.m. Brought Ringo (the Postman) a poem I had written about him. Had a discussion with the locals about the pros & cons of paving the North Fork Rd. – I'm against it. Took Pandora and went to work on the cabin. The Dziuk's (Johnna, Roxanne & Sheryl) came by. I took Sheryl to the post office via snowmobile. Also got my camera and took a few pictures. The sun was out, the skies blue. And the new snow still on the trees. One of the prettiest days since I've been here. It took me all afternoon to finish casing the back window, and to install the sliding windows into the frame. To store for supper with Karen & Bettie. To Hostel to help John Frederic print pictures until the wee morning hours.

Saturday 3/6/82

Lisa called me today – I had left word asking that she call me. It seems she has a boyfriend and wants to quit school. I talked to Helen & her boyfriend's Parents about it yesterday. I am concerned she is heading down the wrong road. She said she had decided to go back to school. I'm concerned that the reason she decided to quit hasn't been taken care of. I feel in talking to her they are still there. She is holding back – not anxious to continue the conversation. This problem will come up again. Took Pandora with me as I do every day. And went to work on the cabin. Worked on the loft window until about 6:00 p.m. Went to the store and cooked Frog legs & crawfish stuffed bell pepper for Karen, Bettie, Ron Wilhelm, and I for supper. Went to the hostel at 7:30 p.m. to a meeting about how to stop the paving of the North Fork road.

Sunday 3/7/82

Loaded the snowmobile in the truck & went to get John Frederik's snowmobile that had been down near the Canadian border. We took a ride into Canada on the snowmobile looking for pictures to take. Late this evening I left John Frederick at the truck to unload the sled we had been pulling. I was going to make a quick run down near the river to take a picture. The sun was below the mountains and it was difficult to see the hills & dips in the snow. All of a sudden I ran up on a small stream crossing in front of me. I hit the brakes but couldn't stop in time. The snowmobile drove nose down into a hole in the snow that was washed out by the stream. I went flying over the handlebars and landed on my hands on the other side of the stream. My

camera was hanging around my neck and under my coat. I took a couple of rolls, but the camera was OK. I got only a couple of scratches on my legs from hitting the handlebars. I was happy that the windshield wasn't on – I had taken it off to put it in the truck. The machine was nose down in the hole and only one way to get it out. I had to lift the entire 450 pounds straight up and pull it back up on the snow some 5 feet up. There was only about 1 foot of water in the stream. After a lot of grunting and groaning I finally got it out. Nothing seemed broken. Tonight I feel the effects of the straining – a muscle in my left arm hurts –and I have a moderate pain in my lower back. Went to Ray Brown's and dropped John Frederick off – then to Phil Sue's place to talk to him about a snowmobile trip and taking his turn at counting cars on the North Fork Rd. for our plans to stop the Northfork paving. Went to Karen and Betties for supper. Got into a lengthy discussion about prejudices. Windy Upton came by Franks about midnight to tell me Joyce O'Hara wants to go skiing with me tomorrow at Big Mountain.

Monday 3/8/82

Up at 7: a.m. Went to O'Hara's but John said Joyce was still sleeping – she came in from playing scrabble at Costello's at 4 a.m. He didn't think she should go skiing. Spent an hour or so on the phone trying to contact a representative of the Sierra Club, and with Mom about some of Dad's legal problems. Went to Costello's and road the kids and grownups on the snowmobile. Went to Philip Sue's on Red Meadow Road. Helped him make a door. We then went up Red Meadow Road on two snowmobiles – his and mine. We had a

great time jumping hills. Running across the frozen red meadow lake, and up the steep mountain overlooking the lake. Found a good steep hill where we could jump 40 or 50 feet. We would run across the frozen snow covered lake at 60 MPH and climb up the 45° side of the mountain until the snowmobile couldn't pull up anymore. Just before it would stop we would turn around and head downhill. There was no stopping and we had to be careful not to get the snowmobile sideways as it would tumble down. Had a couple of burritos at Sue's house and then to have supper with Karen & Bettie.

More letters

Love fuels fight for North Fork

To the editor,

Since when do business types; Chamber of Commerce; bankers; truckers; tourists; recreationists and fuel deliverers have an "interest" in the North Fork?

These "types" have their true interest in only the money that can be obtained from the North Fork area, for their own pockets!

The best reason I can give you as a why these types did not show at the hearing is because 30 years ago (or more), the Highway Department predetermined that the "International Peace Highway" (i.e. the North Fork), would be paved (regardless of local opposition), by the year 2000.

We, the people, have the real interest in the North Fork. Yes, much to your dismay, we are the ecologists; environmentalists; the protectors and residents who see, feel, touch, smell and hear all the beauty of the North Fork and other areas like it.

We are the people who are trying to protect this beauty (what remains) from types concerned more with money and "their" livelihood rather than respect for wilderness inhabitants who were there before you or money!

We aren't cutting up the forests. We aren't making money when the oil and gas companies blow up our backyard. We aren't selling tickets to fish off our land or canoe down the river. We aren't burning coal in our area.

So you may find yourself wondering "why do they oppose?"

I'll let you know. It isn't a great need or desire for money; personal; social or economic gain. It isn't a need to "keep up with the Jones'" either.

It is love. A true respect and love for the Earth Mother. Love for the wilderness and all the living creatures that keep it in harmony, the way it was meant to be.

Perhaps it will not remain this way for long but I am fighting to keep it that way, by any means I am able.

Just how long do you suppose it took the wilderness to earn its livelihood, Ms. Buentemeier? Well, it was a heck of a lot longer than any Flathead business person! Check out your "respect" reservoir, it may be a few quarts low.

Kim Alexander
Columbia Falls

Tuesday 3/9/82

Went to Big Creek Work Center on the North Fork Road to count cars from 9 a.m. to 6 p.m. We are taking turns at this for 10 days to get an idea how far off the statistics are as published for the road paving project. Most of the residents here have banned together to fight the paving the North Fork Road. Stopped by Lee Downes' house to pay him for some lumber, But he wasn't in. Stopped by Tom Ladenburg's to pay him for some logs. To supper with Karen & Bettie. Today I feel bad – think I'm catching something.

Wednesday 3/10/82

Woke up with a sore throat – really don't feel good. Kathlyn Hurst called to talk about the money she put in my account and about things down south. Went to store to get gas but ran out before I got there. Yesterday I ran the truck occasionally to keep warm. It was on the hill and the gauge read incorrectly. Just made it here last night. Had a half gallon of gas at Frank's. Put it in & went to tank up at store. Took the camera and sat near a dead elk carcass near coal Creek. Nothing showed up for 2 hours or so. I was feeling bad, got cold, and decided to leave. Heard a bunch of ravens in the woods. Went to investigate & found a dead deer carcass. The hard winter is taking its toll. To frank's to bake brownies and make Pina Coladas. Took some crawfish stew, etouffee, & stuffed bell peppers over to Ritch Upton's to have dinner there & to watch Karen & Ron Wilhelm on T.V. They were interview about the road paving project. We couldn't get the station they were on. To Frank's to write till midnight.

Thursday 3/11/82

Rainy day – Feel bad – have a cold. Went to work on the cabin. Finished the framing of the loft window. Put linseed oil on the loft floor. And stacked lower floor lumber up in the peak to dry. Cleaned up and went to store for supper with Karen & Bettie. To Frank's to write letter about the road paving & to write other letters for tomorrows mail. To bed 1:30 A.M.

Friday 3/12/82

Went to Post Office, then to work on the cabin. Stained the door and window frames & varnished the side & back walls – took 5 gallons of sealer, varnish and turpentine for this. To Karen and Bettie's for supper. To Frank's to clean up and get things together to go to Kalispell tomorrow. Helen is coming in by plane. Woke up to a heavy snowstorm – 6 to 7 inches of snow on ground. Drove to the airport in Kalispell. Stopped by and talked to John Frederick – he was counting cars at Big Creek. Also stopped a little further down the road to help Joyce O'Hara out of the snow berm. The snow had packed under her fender and had locked her right wheel. Picked Helen up at 12:35 p.m. Went to Kalispell to get supplies, run errands, and wash cloths. Arrived at Frank's cabin about 6:00 p.m. Stopped by Big Creek to give John Frederic his camera I had picked up for him. Started losing my voice late this evening. I have had a slight cold for nearly a week now.

'Hippies, yippies' oppose N.F. paving

To the editor,

Why is it that there are a certain bunch of nincompoops around Polebridge who have to be against making the North Fork in good shape?

That road is terrible right now. No one likes to drive the cotton-picking road in the very bad condition it is in. And no one but a bunch of hippies and yippies and a few others up there are trying their darndest to keep the North Fork from being black-topped and graded.

If they don't like the paving idea, they should get back out of the North Fork for good and find themselves work instead of being on food stamps and welfare checks!

I am all for grading and black-topping the road all the way to the Canadian border.

I suggest that you opponents get out of the picture entirely.

Daniel Clarkson
Polson

'Paving road won't hurt wildlife'

To the editor,

This is in response to the paving of the North Fork Road.

People say don't do it because there isn't enough travel. Well, many people wouldn't, and don't drive on that poor excuse of a road because of what it does to their vehicles. Why was a new $250,000 border station built last year, if there wasn't enought travel? Then that shouldn't have been built. The old one was adequate.

Paving the road certainly isn't going to hurt the wildlife. It didn't do any harm in Glacier Park.

It's easy for the people who don't have to drive the road everyday to say don't pave it. Many people work up the North Fork, and have to drive it everyday. It does a lot of damage to their vehicles.

They should pave the road for a 35 MPH speed limit. That wouldn't hurt anything.

Mr. & Mrs. Randy Rosenbaum
Columbia Falls

Sunday 3/14/82

Have laryngitis today – can't talk. Don't really feel that bad though. Took Helen Riding on the snowmobile. Went to the cabin for a while, visited Costello's, Went cross country to Doug Chadwick's – Spent most of the day on the snowmobile. Went to the ranger station to make arrangements to go skiing at Big Mountain tomorrow. Frank Evans called late tonight from Colorado. He said he will visit with Genny there and will be back here in a couple of weeks.

Monday 3/15/82
Weather stormy and snowing. Went to Rich Upton's, O'Hara's & Wilhelm's to call off the skiing trip. Stayed inside today Defleshed four of the deer hides I have to tan

Tues 3/16/82
Helen and I worked on the cabin today. Varnished the inside walls of the cabin. Stained the loft window. Made a trash can by hollowing out a log with the chain saw.

Photo of ice on pine needles

Wednesday 3/17/82

Got up at 7:30 a.m. to go skiing at big Mountain. Listened to the weather forecast on the way. The weather was bad and getting worse. Decided to do some chores instead – brought chain saw in to have blades sharpened and to have the bar hammered. Looked for wood stove for cabin, bought boots for Helen, got estimate on truck, bought more varnish etc. Went to meet a bunch of people from Polebridge at Mountain Shadows at 5:30 p.m. Checked in Hotel in Columbia Falls. Helen stayed there to wash her hair while I went to the elementary school for a meeting on paving the North Fork Road. It lasted till midnight. We all (Polebridge bunch) went to a bar, The Bandit till 1:30 a.m. Lisa didn't go to school today. I was upset with her and called her to insist that she go to school. She said she would.

Thursday 3/18/82

Woke up to blowing snow – no skiing for today. Went to Kalispell to check out a stove. Went to library, went grocery shopping and bought me plastic plates to make skies for a chicken. (I will try to get pictures of a chicken skiing. Called Lisa – she hadn't gone to school yesterday. I am very upset with her for lying to me and everyone else. Went back to the North Fork – Saw 20 or so deer. Went to the cabin to drop off supplies and get the acid to make the formula to tan hides.

Friday 3/19/82

Helen and I worked on cabin today. Hung the curtains my mother had made, put acid on the hides after they were stretched and nailed to the floor. Varnished frames of windows and the log trash can. Went to Costello's to visit  a minuet. Ended up having tacos and playing rummy till 1:30 A.M.

Saturday 3/20/82
Today is the first day of spring – and ironically, it's snowing. We went to cabin to put more formula on the deer and elk hides. Made a 7' snowman. To Costello's to visit and to get a key to his place. He'll be in Chicago for 3 months. Went to Karen and Bettie's for dinner at 5:30 p.m. Frank had come in and was there also. Jerry De Santo stopped by & we all had a spaghetti & meatball supper. Went to the Hostel for a meeting about the North Fork Road.

Sunday 3/21/82
Frank Vitale came by and we worked on shoveling the snow off of Frank's cabin (the one he moved from the boarder). The weight had cracked the rafters. Helen & I took the Snowmobile up Hay Creek, Cyclone Mountain, and Spruce Creek – 36 miles. Helen was tired to we went back to frank's by late afternoon. She fixed a tostado casserole for supper. Her stomach was upset – probably from riding the snowmobile she thought.

302

Monday 3/22/82

Frank fixed his homemade huckleberry pancakes for breakfast. We went to Big Mountain to go skiing with some of the people from the North Fork. Helen called Lisa – She hadn't gone to school. Had used Helen's charge card to charge gas etc. Ate all the food for the week (fed her friends). I was so angry with her I could bite the bark off the trees. Helen was upset too and wanted to go home. We didn't ski. Couldn't get a plane out today and her departure was from Calgary, Canada – 100 or so cheaper than from Kalispell.

Helen arranged for Lisa to go to my mothers. I was to take Helen through Lake Louise, Banff and on to Calgary. Drove into Canada and to Lake Louise. Saw several elk eating the grass alongside the road in Ca. Took a picture of a bull elk just as he was running toward the truck. Went to Lake Louise – it was frozen over, the chalet was closed and everything was white – Not pretty like in the summer. Drove on to Banff. Looked around the area there –

snowing heavily. Bow Falls was frozen solid. Shopped around Banff most of the afternoon. Drove in a snowstorm to the airport in Calgary Alberta Canada. Shopped a little for some curtain rings. Helen bought a couple of souvenirs at the airport and got on her flight home at 12:30 p.m. I drove on to a small town 25 miles east of Calgary to get a windshield for my snowmobile. It was a tinted one and I hadn't been able to find one in the U.S. Drove on to Columbia Falls, Mt. Took pictures of some Canada Geese just south of the border. The road was small, windy, steep and snow packed for several miles to Saint Mary. Followed Highway 2 east instead of Highway 2 west to Browning to a little past Cut Bank before I realized my mistake. Drove 70 or so miles for nothing. Got over the pass and into Columbia Falls by 12 Midnight. Parked at the Night Owl Restaurant and slept in the truck

Thursday 3/25/82
Got gas – I was empty. Drove on to Lakeside just south of Kalispell to check out some wood burning stoves. One was too small, the other too large. Bought a set of 8 ply tires (new) from a guy for $250.00. Had two of them mounted on the front end (they were bald). I wanted to align the front end, but found out I had worn tie rods & king pins. The mechanic gave me an estimate of $335.00. I decided to fix it myself. Paid $75.00 for the tie rod ends – will fix king pins when I get a reamer. Drove on to the North Fork. Took pictures of Deer on the way up.

Friday 3/26/82
Frank and I cut firewood all morning. Got mail and wrote letters till 2:30 p.m. Went to Frank Vitale's on Red Meadow Road to borrow a sprayer from him. Sprayed ½ of the cabin ceiling with linseed oil before dark. Today was a pretty sunshiny day.

Saturday 3/27/82
Pat called this morning. Talked for an hour or so. Frank went into town for the day. Cut some firewood, varnished cabin walls & back window. Sprayed linseed oil on loft floor, put neatsfoot oil on the hides, cut and pulled support log for ridgepole, & began cutting trees for railings. Went to Tom Reamer's to see if a group of them still plan to go on a cross country ski trip tomorrow. Fell on a hole in his driveway and was stuck for an hour. Today was a pretty day also.

Sunday 3/28/82

Did some writing, organized some pictures I was to send to Pat, washed dishes, and baked a cake. Went to Dziuk's to invite them to supper. Kathlyn Hurst had brought some crawfish stew for them. Worked on cutting trees and peeling them for the loft railing. Brought them over to Frank's and hung them to dry over the stove. Fixed supper, and had the Dziuk's over about dark. Cleaned kitchen and wrote till midnight.

Monday 3/29/82

Called Helen – Lisa left home. She didn't want to go to school, or behave herself. Helen told her to leave again. She packed and went stay with her friend Linda. I told Helen to get the papers arranged to give me custody. I will try to do something to correct the situation when I get back. Felt very sad about this all day. Worked on cabin. Put another coat of linseed oil below the loft floor. Stuffed fiberglass insulation between some of the logs, and cut the rest of the railing pickets. To Frank's about dark to eat and write till midnight. The problem waiting for me when I return to Lafayette seem unduly heavy. I feel I am preparing to go to jail for something I didn't do

Tuesday 3/30/82

Spent the morning on the telephone, washing dishes, writing letters and cleaning the glass on the back windows of the log cabin. After dinner I went to work on the cabin. Installed the back windows and sealed them with weather-stripping. Cut the post that fits between the ridgepoles & loft and acts to support the snow on the roof. Fastened the three posts to the loft floor with lag bolts. Cut the two 5 ½ trees I will use to make the ladder to the loft. Drug them from the Dziuk's property to the driveway. To Frank's after dark. Cooked brownies for tomorrow's pot luck supper. Wrote till 11 p.m. Felt very down today about the problem back home.

Wednesday 3/31/82

Worked with Frank cutting next winter's firewood. We worked till about 2 p.m. – brought in about 3 chords of wood to his house. Have another 3 chords cut in the woods. It began snowing heavily just as we were quitting. Snowed about 4" today. Changed all of the tie rods & linkage on the truck. I got soaking wet and the weather was turning cold with a North wind. Finished about 5 p.m. Took a bath and went to a pot luck supper – meeting set up to talk about the coal mine planned to be put in just north of the border.

Thursday 4/1/82

Spent a couple of hours catching up on some reading. The propane lights at night aren't very bright and are hard on my eyes. Frank went to Fernie British Columbia to a meeting with the Canadians about trying to stop the coal mine. I decided not to go. I don't have much time left here, and have other things I want to do. Met Ray brown on the way to the cabin. Took him to Red Meadow Road. Went to the cabin and put another coat of linseed oil on the ceiling. Lit the stove, picked up (untacked) the tanned deer & elk hides. Drug in and peeled the two poles I will use for the loft ladder. Cleaned the picture window with a razor blade. I was disappointed that the other razor blade I had used had scratched the window in places. An eagle came by this afternoon and perched on the old snag in front of the cabin. To Frank's after dark – read & wrote till midnight. Kevin called today. He wants me to pay him some of the child support. He is having financial problems and owes & 400.00. I'm not sure if he thinks I owe this to him or if he is generally asking for help. Not sure if he has learned the value of money or if he still thinks people have to give it to him. Not sure what I should do. I need more information.

North Fork

by H. Frank Evans

Snow, snow, snow. It has scarcely missed a day since the month April was born and there is still a two-foot depth of the stuff left from winter's doing. The other day we had a thunderstorm while the white stuff fell. One day the flakes blow almost horizontal on a north wind and the next day the direction is reversed.

Nights are still cold enough to make it crisp under foot in the mornings but the total structure makes for intrepid walking. One goes a few feet on top of the crust and then comes a step that descends to ground level as the crust gives way. This is always accompanied by an unprintable expletive. I'm impatient and want nothing to slow my progress from here to there.

I've always been an advocate of getting next winter's wood supply in March but seldom have I managed to accomplish the task — just too many things to do. However, this year I believe the job is done. With Jim Hale's good help we felled and sectioned some crisp dry lodgepole pines, big ones, that grew at roadside. But since only the driveway is void of snow, the tremendous heap of wood is in a formless pile on the north side of the cabin.

When the snow has finally melted, I shall split and haul the tons of wood and stack it in the woodshed. That is a wheelbarrowing job and it will be good before-breakfast work for several weeks. Getting one's own wood is supposed to warm one twice but handling it so many times warms one too many times. One fells the trees, bucks it up, stacks it in the truck, unloads it, and then it will be split, stacked in the wheelbarrow, pushed to the shed and stacked again. Whew!

There's one thing good about cutting one's own wood, it is a free, untaxable income.

And the energy comes not from splitting atoms but from splitting molecules. The complex molecules of cellulose and lignin were put together with the energy of sunlight and that same energy is released in combustion. It is fossil sunshine the same as coal or oil. It is certainly a very positive asset that comes from being a forest dweller.

On the 15th there were almost 40 of us assembled at the hostel for a pot luck dinner and to hear Ron Cooper give a complete rundown on the Flathead River Environmental Study which has been federally funded and was precipitated by the pending threat of the Cabin Creek coal mine. A decision by the British Columbia government will decide in the near future whether or not Sage Creek Coal Co. can proceed with its plans to mine the coal a very few miles above the international border.

Friday 4/2/82

Light snow in the morning. Cleaned house, washed dishes & went for mail. Back to Frank's with Johnna Dziuk. Cleaned the fins and air passageways around the chainsaw cylinder & head. They were stopped up with wood chips etc. and would cause the saw to overheat when it was worked hard. Took Johnna to her house and worked on cabin. Cut the steps for the ladder and pealed them. Paula and Johnna Dziuk came over for a while. Cut the hole in the floor for the trapdoor. Lit the stove. Dug 2 rolls of tarpaper I will use as a moisture barrier between the sub floor and the finished floor. Put them by the stove to warm up. Cut up the extra poles around the cabin to use as firewood. Trimmed the trees in front so they wouldn't block the view from the loft window. Fitted the first floor board to the wall log. To Frank's about 8 p.m. to eat and make a pair of goggles for a chicken we will dress up for skiing. Will call it the "Chicken Skier". And photograph it to use perhaps as a poster or on a tee shirt. Temperature is dropping tonight -16°F by 10 p.m.

Saturday 4/3/82

Frank and I spent the morning cutting next year's firewood and hauling it to his cabin. Started laying the finished floor on the cabin. Chuck and Johnna came over for a while. Stopped at 4:00 p.m. To Hostel for a shower then picked up Karen Feather and went to Kalispell. We washed our cloths and did a little grocery shopping. Had a pizza and went dancing. Left Kalispell at 2 a.m. in a blizzard. The drifting snow along the North Fork Road. Was as pretty as I've seen it. The snow blowing from one direction and another was entrancing – had to drive slowly. Arrived at Polebridge sometime after 3:30

Sunday 4/4/82

Loaded the snowmobile in the truck and drove to Red Meadow Road. Glade Young borrowed Peggy Gensler's snowmobile and we road up Moose Creak Road and several other roads branching off. Found a good hill to climb with several jumps. Took pictures with each other's camera. We found an old abandoned log cabin back in the woods. Looked around, jumped on roof into snow and took pictures for half hour or so. Got in a snowstorm so heavy we could hardly drive. Stopped by and had tea with Patty Petite and Mary Jane who were visiting from Alaska. Patty has a cabin near Moose Creak Road. Got to Frank's about 9 p.m. He fixed a scrumptious Cornish game hen dinner. WE ate about 10 p.m. I had an enjoyable day today. Riding the snowmobile tired me out.

Monday 4/5/82

Up. 6. a.m. – Picked up Mary and Pat at 7:30 a.m. Drove them to Whitefish and met Rich Upton, Jerry Desanto, John O'Hara at Big Mountain for a day of skiing. Mary and Pat joined us later. Rich helped me with some pointers. He was an instructor and on ski patrol in Lake Tahoe for several years. I skied with them all afternoon.

Skied all lifts including the black slopes. Took a few falls and got a slight sprain in my right ankle. We had a few drinks and went to Whitefish to have supper at Coupe De Ville restaurant. Took Bettie back to Polebridge with me. Got home about 10:30 p.m. Had a good day

Tuesday 4/6/82F

Spent the morning washing dishes. Making Phone call to Mom & Helen about Lisa, reading & writing letters for mail today. Worked on putting down more flooring in the cabin until dark. Went to Frank Vitale's to get a chicken.

Wednesday 4/7/82

Worked all morning making goggles for the chicken. I had made skis, poles, suspenders and a scarf for it. By afternoon Frank helped me get some pictures of the "chicken Skier" Took the bantam rooster back to Frank Vitale's. Found Lynx tracks along the berm on the way to his house. Pandora had a thrill chasing a fool hen. Back to Frank's to eat and do some reading and writing until 11 p.m.

Thursday 4/8/82

Got up with Frank and we had waffles for breakfast. He went to Kalispell for the day. Went to the cabin to put down more flooring. Ran out of lumber just 2 feet short of the wall. Packed some fiberglass insulation in the cracks between the logs. Several coyotes were howling a chorus just below the cabin. Pandora was all ears, but kept quiet. Frank came back home about 10:30 p.m. Wrote letters for tomorrow's mail.

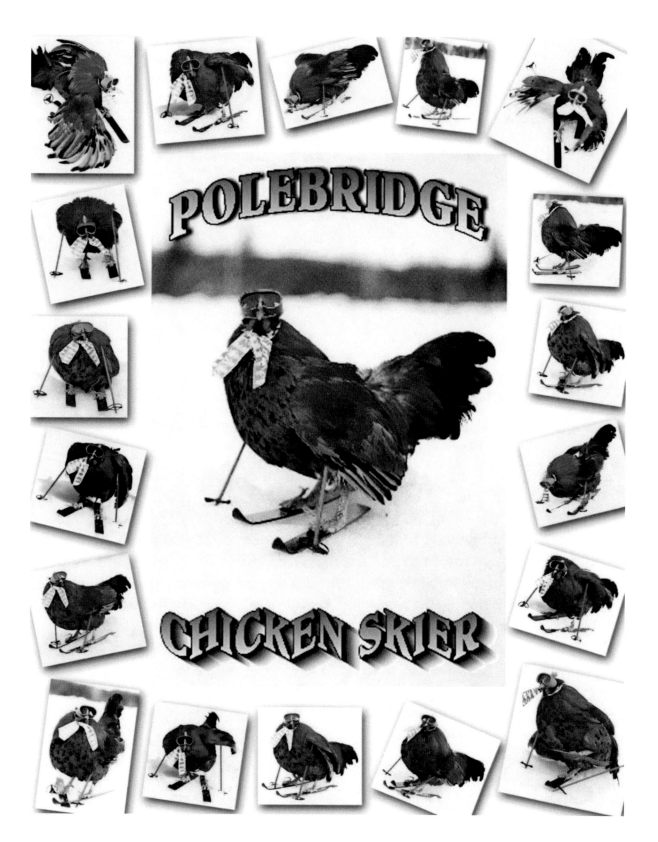

Friday 4/9/82

Up around 7 a.m. Frank and I cut firewood all day. Joe Mahurin came over later and helped us. We loaded and stacked about 10 chords on the side of frank's house. He thinks he now has enough for next winter. My next chore is to cut Karen's firewood for next winter. They have both been good to me and this is something I want to do for them. Just before dark I loaded the snowmobile in the truck and went to get 5 dozen eggs from Glade Young who was staying at Peggy Gensler's house while she was away. Bettie & Karen came over and had dinner (supper) with Frank, Joe, & I. Bettie said Rodney Savoy had called with a message that Mike Norse had died.

Saturday 4/10/82

For some unknown reason I feel good today. Possibly it was because of all the hard work I did yesterday. Weather is a warm 30° and sunny today. However there is still a storm system near Yellowstone in Wyoming. I may have to cancel my plans to go there unless it clears soon. The elk are beginning to lose their racks and the pictures I plan to take won't be as interesting. Called

Rodney this afternoon to ask that he order some flowers for Mike Norse's funeral. Also called Phil Norse Sr. – he is taking it hard. Phil Jr. wasn't there but called later. He broke down on the phone and couldn't finish the conversation. It's just so hard and sad – I don't like funerals. Thought about my Dad – It will be strange for me to go back home and get used to him not being around. Mike was only 42 -2 years older than I – he died of cancer. Went to cabin to finish stuffing fiberglass in the cracks between the logs over the loft, to put another coat of linseed oil on the ceiling, and to put a coat of linseed on half the lower floor. Frank Evans and Joe Mahurin came by to visit. Also Frank Vitale and Ellen Horwity (his wife) came by to visit. Bill Brown and a friend of his came by for me to move my truck so he could get by on the road. He had been fixing broken water pipes in his cabin for the last 2 days. To Frank's about dark to eat take a bath and write.

Sunday 4/11/82

Up 7:30 – a miserable Rainey day – not what we would like to see on Easter Sunday. Spent most of the day cutting down trees that could fall on one of Frank's cabins, putting up the crank telephone line that the snowplow knocked down and trimming the trees that touched the line. Tried to get the phone working, but couldn't – needed a voltmeter. Changed out of my wet cloths and helped Frank with supper – washed dishes. Karen & Bettie came over and we had alligator tail as the main dish. Kathlyn Hurst had brought it up from Louisiana on her last trip. We all played "Oh Hell" till late.

Monday 4/12/82

Frank and Joe went to Kalispell. I went to work on making railings on the loft. Finished about 1½ sections of railing – this is a slow job. Went to have supper with Karen, Bettie, Frank, Joe Mahurin, & John Frederick at the store. Played "Oh Hell" again until 11 p.m.

Tuesday 4/13/82

A nasty rainy day today. Went to mail letter and get mail. Helen called – Lisa was suspended from school today for being insulting to a teacher. I can't seem to do much about the situation from over here. Lisa is fast becoming a psychological problem and may very well end up in trouble with the law if things aren't reversed soon. At minimum she will become (or has already become) a social problem. Don't get any input from her so I can only get an outward view of what could be her underlying problem. I am not surprised, but very disturbed about her direction. Took the Dziuk kids to their house, and went to work on the loft railings. Would have finished with this today, but bored a hole in the wrong place on one of the railings and will have to cut another tree down and dry it. Started working on the loft ladder. To Frank's by dark. Mike Ross had worked with Frank on one of his cabins today. He had supper and stayed the night

Wednesday 4/14/82

Called Helen – Lisa left home again yesterday – her boyfriend, Lance came to pick her up. A rainy day again. Went to cabin and built the ladder to the loft. Roxanne helped me till dark – finished the ladder. Pat called and talked for most of an hour. Frank had supper ready just as she called. He left and went outside – didn't come back for about 2 hours.

Thursday 4/15/82

Today the spring bear season opens – not many bears out yet though. Still have over 2 feet of snow on the ground. Spent the morning washing dishes and cleaning house. Went to work on the cabin. Chuck and Johnna came by. They sanded the railings while I made the trap door. Cleaned the floors and sprayed the ceiling with linseed oil on the ceiling (2nd coat) also put another coat of linseed oil on the loft floor and half the lower floor. Varnished the railings, the ladder, and 2 walls. Went to Frank's about dark. There was a "Pot Luck" supper at the Hostel and a speaker there with the Flathead River basin study. I went there, had supper and took a shower. Karen told me Frank had fallen in his border cabin and hurt his back. He fell on a full can of paint, and mashed the can splattering white paint over everything. There was a display of the Northern lights as I was leaving the Hostel. The night was crystal clear – Beautiful.

317

Friday 4/16/82

Went for mail – then to cabin to put a coat of varnish on the wall and to cut a couple of poles for curtain rods. Johnna came with me. Back to Frank's to have a sandwich, pack and leave for Missoula Mt. Frank and I were going to the 5th annual wildlife film festival at the University of Montana. He took his car as he was going to Colorado after the festival. I was to go to Yellowstone to photograph elk. Exchanged the non-tinted snowmobile windshield for some injection oil. Took the east side of Flathead Lake & arrived in Missoula about 7:00 p.m. Spent nearly an hour locating the room where the festival films were shown. Watched film until midnight. Unrolled my sleeping bag & slept in the cab of the truck in a parking lot at the university.

Saturday 4/17/82

Up about 7 a.m. – Had the rear tires changed on the truck. Put on 2 of the 8 ply tires I had bought earlier. Went to the festival to watch film, attended a reception at the University lounge, and sat in the workshop on Wildlife Photography. This is an international wildlife film festival, but I'm not overly impressed at the quality of the films. Nor am I impressed with the knowledge and organization of the filmmakers. This field seems to be only crudely developed as in the primary stage. There are only parts that seem refined. Much of the contents of the films are the easy shots – lots of bird pictures – only a small part of the hard to get shots of predators or like animals. The snapshot wildlife display and contest was really a disappointment – poor in quality. Only a few seemed professional. Because of this festival I feel more confident in displaying my work in competition. Also learned that few wildlife filmmakers are showing a profit. Slept in truck.

Sunday 4/18/82

Up at 8:00 – went for breakfast and to watch more film till about 2:30 p.m. Found a laundromat and washed my cloths. Frank didn't come to the festival today – he left for Colorado this a.m. Drove to west Yellowstone, Wyoming. Arrived about 1 a.m. – slept in truck.

Photo of Ice on Glass

Monday 4/19/82

Temperature last night dropped to 15° below zero. The inside of the windows had a thick layer of frost on them. Had breakfast about 7 a.m. & went into Yellowstone Park. Got several pictures of elk, deer, and ducks & Canadian geese. Weather began to cloud by noon. Had some snow. Drove down to old Faithful and back up to Gardner, Mountain. Lots of deer & elk in poor shape – some look like walking dead. Lots of snow still on the ground too. It's been a hard winter for them. Many will die within the next month before the grass turns green and food is available. Slept in the truck near Gardner.

Tuesday 4/20/82

Temp was 5 below zero last night. Had breakfast and went into the park by 7 a.m. Drove to Cooke city and back to Gardner. Got a couple shots of a coyote & several good ones of a big moose. Have found two dead deer, a dead buffalo, and 4 dead elk – and really haven't been stomping the woods much. Also found, between Mammoth Hot Springs &Gardner, a place where hot springs mixes with a stream. The water is just nice for swimming. Tried to track a coyote today & slid down a muddy hill – had to change my pants. Spent several hours looking for bighorn sheep between Mammoth Hot Springs & Gardner. Today was a beautiful sunny day – very unusual they say, as there's been bad weather here for weeks. I guess I got lucky. My face is a little red & my eyes burn – snowburn. On my way back I

saw the most deer I have ever seen in one area in a 25 mile stretch just north of Gardner, Wyoming. A conservative estimate would be 700, but perhaps as many as 1,000. And I didn't stop to glass the hills – these were just seen while driving. Most herds were between 10 & 20 deer, but many were over 50. Counted 63 in one herd. Deer were scattered everywhere. Must be a wintering area. The deer didn't seem as poor as those in Yellowstone. Drove on to Missoula, Montana – arrived 1:30 a.m. Slept in the truck at the University there.

Wednesday 4/21/82
Up at 6:30 a.m. Drove to the National Bison Range and got some shots of Antelope. Didn't see many bison, and no elk. Drove on to Kalispell. Spent the afternoon getting supplies. Went to a campground on highway 2 and took a much needed shower. Spent an hour or so at the Post Office writing letters and getting off my last roll of film. Went to Bill Brown's to visit until 11:30 p.m. Drove to an apartment complex where I slept in the truck in a back parking lot.

Thursday 4/22/82

Finished getting supplies this morning. My lumber wasn't ready yet. Drove on to the North Fork. Walked around Camas Creek and on Glacier park side for a couple of hours. I was looking for deer antlers to use as a door handle for the cabin. Found just what I wanted – a right hand antler just the right size. Unloaded things at Frank's and at my cabin. The weather was warm and the snow was melting fast. There was water over Frank's driveway when I came in – the creek is beginning to overflow. Frank called later this night from Colorado – said he'll be back middle of next week.

Friday 4/23/82
Spent most of the morning putting away my things, sharpening plane blade, fixing chain saw oiler, getting my mail ready, etc. The Dziuk's came over for a ride up to their house. Went for my mail, then with the Dziuk's to the cabin. Worked on bolting the ladder to the floor and stuffing fiberglass between the logs. Chuck and Johnna painted linseed oil on the outside. Melted down a large bucket of beef fat and poured it into an old tree snag in front of cabin. Should attract birds, small animals and maybe a bear. To Frank's about dark. Karen came over just as I was trying to get across a pond of water to Frank's house. The stream was raging louder than I had heard it before. Had to wade across 2 foot deep icy water to get to the cabin. Pandora wouldn't cross and I had to go back & carry her across. Karen and I had made with Rockefeller sauce – excellent

Saturday 4/24/82
Used Frank's boat to get across the overflowing stream this morning. To store to get pictures that were part of yesterday's mail. To cabin to stuff fiberglass between logs. Did this most of the day. Also replaced broken glass on back window, varnished the last section of wall, nailed my wooden axe (ornament) to the gable end and began spraying linseed oil on outside of cabin just as I was leaving to Frank's to take a bath and write till midnight.

Sunday 4/25/82
Sketched the lining to the curtains this morning – spent 4 hours doings this. Went to Polebridge store to meet Karen's sister & husband. Went to cabin and finished stuffing fiberglass between the logs. Also finished putting together the last railing on the left. Cut down several small trees to make a couple of frames to stretch coon skins on. Roughed out 4 ends for curtain rods. To Frank's to make frames for coon skins. Peeled the sticks by candlelight outside. Also finished the ends for the curtain rods (brackets) and stained them. To bed sometime in the wee morning hours.

Monday 4/26/82

Ron Wilhelm came over and woke me up at 9:30 a.m. Kirt Jenkins came over to use the phone. Went to work on the cabin. Johnna and Paula came over and helped. We cleaned everything off the floor. Set up stove to get some heat up to dry the varnish and linseed oil. It was drying slowly. Put up curtain rods. Sanded and varnished railings, ladder & curtain rods. Made frame for door. To Dziuk's at 6 p.m. to have supper with them and play cards. To Frank's to untangle a huge ball of string & to write till midnight.

Tuesday 4/27/82
Up 7:30 a.m. Washed dishes & cleaned house. Went to Polebridge ranger station to talk to Jerry De Santo. He had found a tree where a bear had made a den. I wanted to photograph the bear with her cubs. Went to store to get mail. Took Dziuk's to their house, had some gingerbread there and went to work on cabin. Chuck came with me. Lit fire in stove. Sanded and painted railing, ladder curtain rods. Fitted trap door and put hinges & handle on it. Went down ridge to look for a large tree for a step. Came back & put sealer under ½ of the floor. Decided to make a round window in the door & use a log end for the frame (to resemble a hollow log). Made frame for this. To Frank's to eat, cut glass for the door window, write & to bed midnight.

Wednesday 4/28/82

 Frank called from Kalispell. He was on his way back to Colorado. Was to be back from North Fork this afternoon. Went to cut a step out of a large Tamarack tree near Jerry Costello's. Spent a good part of the morning doing this. I wasn't satisfied with it and abandoned the project for now. Went to the cabin and began cleaning the front half of the floor. Put a coat of linseed oil on it. Lit the fire & went outside to begin digging a hole for an outhouse. It had rained all afternoon and was raining pretty hard. I decided to quit early & go have supper with Frank. He eats early, while I usually work till dark. Nearly 3' of water between Frank's and the road. I used his boat. After supper I worked making some little critters out of the tree branches I had collected.

Thursday 4/29/82

Woke up to a white world – snow again. It seems winter doesn't want to quit. Frank says he's never seen so much snow on the ground by this time of year, nor has he seen water up so high for so long. Went to cabin to put some aluminum heat shields on one of the purling logs near the stove pipe. Lit the fire and went to Frank's With Chuck to return his ladder. Began cutting firewood for Karen in an area that Frank wanted to clear so he could have a view of the mountains. The bearings on the bar sprocket went out on the chain saw. Went to store to borrow Karen's and bring my shovel to Wilhelm so he could weld a break in it for me. Cut wood until about 5:30. Took Chuck back. Bettie, her youngest daughter, and her husband came over to see the cabin, Back to Frank's to eat. Cut wood & burned the slash till 10:30 p.m. Stained coon skin frames, wrote & to bed midnight.

Friday 4/30/82

 Didn't sleep much last night. I feel like a race horse coming into the last straight away to the finish line. Lots left to do and will be counting days from 5/1/82. Did chores, went for mail, and took a few pictures – weather is pretty. Took Dziuk's back to their house and went to work on the cabin. Paula & Johnna came with me. Put lag bolts in ladder, cleaned loft floor & put another coat of linseed oil on the loft floor & ½ of bottom floor. Paula and I went to Frank's & cut firewood for Karen until about 6:00 p.m. Took her back home and returned to cut more firewood till dark. Had supper with Frank & Mark Rose. Began stretching a coonskin on a frame – got sleepy & went to bed 10:30 p.m.

Saturday 5/1/82

Today is another pretty sunshiny day, but it looks like it may get misty & cloud up. Have had a few sunny days. Decided the day taking pictures of outhouse to maybe make a little book. Picked up Chuck Dziuk & went to border. Took a roll of film along the way. Found an old car with wooden spoked wheel at Moose City. We were able to get 3 of the wheels off. Took them home with us. Went to a birthday party for Bettie at the Polebridge store. There were perhaps 30 people there. Played volleyball till dark. To bed 11:30 or so.

Outhouse at Jimmy Little"s cabin
(Below Costello's cabin)

Sunday 5/2/82

Took Pandora to cabin and then went down to the ridge to the cabin known as rat haven – took a picture of an old outhouse there. Had my 300 Weatherby mag so decided to walk to the river to see if any bear had been around. We had walked for an hour or so – Pandora had chased after a couple of deer and sent one swimming the river to the park side. She wouldn't bark but would just take off running when she would see something. I kept an eye on her as she would sniff around. I noticed her lingering around one spot for a long time. I went over and found she

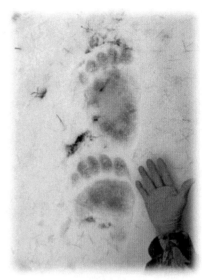

was on a bear scent. We found where it crossed the snow since daylight. It was about 10 am so I knew there was a bear around – a grizzly. His footprint was a ½" longer than my boot – 12 ¾" and considerably wider. The claw marks extended another 3 ½". We trailed it, but Pandora kept well ahead of me and searched back and forth a lot. She is good to have along because of her nose, but she spooks everything ahead of me. I was sneaking along a small stream when she suddenly too off across a meadow. I ran up out of the stream bed just in time to see the silver-grey grizzly running for the trees on

the other side of the meadow. The sun was shining on it & its' muscles flexing shone in ripples across the hair. It was the first grizzly had seen up here, and it appeared to me to be a big one. We trailed for a while, but soon gave up. The bear knew we were on her trail, and we wouldn't see it again. Searched awhile for coyote tracks, and then climbed back up to the cabin. Pandora was tired from all her hunting – so was I. Worked on digging an outhouse hole – finished about 5 p.m. Went to Frank's for supper. Went out after supper and cut down trees for firewood for 2 hours or so. Took a bath, wrote, & to bed 11p.m.

Whitefish Lake

Monday 5/3/82

Picked up Chuck, Johnna & Roxanne Dziuk and went to Kalispell to get supplies, run errands and get groceries. Went to Superior Lumber. Karen was there with her truck. Since my truck was loaded with 35 cases of beer for the store. I loaded my lumber on her truck. We stopped along the way to the North Fork and looked for deer antlers for ½ hour or so. Arrived in North Fork about 6:30 p.m. Went out to cut wood on Frank's land about 7 p.m. Pat called and talked for an hour or so. She had recently gone to the hospital. Frank reprimanded me for being on the phone for so long – he sure has been uptight lately. I needed to make another call but was so aggravated I went over to the store to use the pay phone – it was out of order. I guess I'll have to be rude to friends who call just to talk – will have to cut them short. It's not my phone – a privilege that I even have one available I guess.

Tuesday 5/4/82

Up 6 a.m. Drove to Columbia Falls to call Jane Brown & cancel Joyce O'Hara and my plans to go horseback riding today. Went to Whitefish to try to locate Leo Mc Donald, the guy who backed into my truck at the Polebridge store. Found that he had moved to Oregon & worked in the Oil business in Utah. Called his wife and spoke to her about the problem I was having with their insurance Company. Went to small claims court to file a suit, but found out the courts in Montana have no jurisdiction to serve him in Oregon – a legal stumbling block. Called Helen – couldn't find Kevin at home – I wanted to talk to him. Mom not home either, but Helen says she is doing O.K. Ran a few errands and back to North Fork about 5 p.m., Cut firewood till 10 p.m.

Wednesday 5/5/82

Spent the day making the cabin door and putting it up. Went to Kirt and Patty Jenkins for supper. Made curtain rings out of rope.

Thursday 5/6/82

Made moldings for door and also a threshold. Cut out and installed door lock. Put on deer antler door handle. To Hostel at 4 p.m. to shower. Picked up tom Reimer at 5 p.m. and went to Columbia Falls to eat with several others from Polebridge and to bowl till 11 p.m. Back to North Fork by midnight. I'm losing my voice and don't feel good – catching something.

Friday 5/7/82
Woke up with a cold. Got mail and went to cabin. Moved deer antler handle. It was too close to the door Jam. Stained door. Put down flooring. Chuck came over to help. An eagle perched on the big tamarack snag in front of the cabin for ½ hour or so. Must be one of the same two that frequently come by and sit on that tree. Cut the dead lodgepole from around the cabin to help keep away any forest fires that may come along.

Saturday 5/8/82
I feel weak today – have a cold. To cabin to finish fitting the last piece of flooring against the wall. Put a coat of linseed oil on the newly laid floor and front half of bottom floor – also on outside of door. Varnished inside of door. Sealed under the cabin with wood preserver. To Frank's to cut firewood for Karen for an hour and a half. Had supper about 7 p.m. Went out after supper to cut more firewood till 9:30 p.m. When I go to bed at night lately I think of how Pandora will do when I leave. Each night when I lie down to get in my sleeping bag she comes over for me to rub her neck and ears for a minute. Then she will lick my face once, and go to sleep. It's as though she needs that last touch of affection before she goes to sleep. She is also saying good night to me in her own way. I will miss her – she is with me everywhere I go. We have become as close as man and dog can be and seem to understand each other. Hope she will make the adjustment back to Frank without much trouble. Today she saw something near the cabin and got really excited. She barked with a disturbing tone. I grabbed the gun and jumped out of the cabin. I didn't see anything but she sniffed each little twig and leaf just as she did when she encountered the grizzly. I can only assume that she had seen a bear – she doesn't act this way with anything else.

Sunday 5/9/82
Spent a couple hours this morning cutting Karen's firewood. Spent a couple more hours helping Frank swap refrigerators in his rent cabin. Went to my cabin and lit a fire in the stove. Cut more dead lodgepole from around the cabin, stacked and burned brush until supper time at 7 p.m. Karen came over to visit for 15 minutes or so just as I was getting ready to leave. Back after supper to cut stock and burn trees till 10:30 p.m. Washed up & to bed about midnight.

Monday 5/10/82
Couldn't sleep last night. Felt bad from the cold and stayed awake thinking about

all I have to do before I left here, and all I have to face when I get back to LA. Got up about 7:30 am & had breakfast. I was still tired. Frank left for town and I fell asleep in the beanbag for a couple of hours. Got up and went to the cabin to finish clearing trees from around the cabin and burning the brush. I felt weak – just don't have my strength. Went to Frank's around 6 p.m. to straighten up and help with supper. We were having a dinner for Bettie. Her birthday was 5/1/82 and this was her present. Karen and Bettie came over about 7 p.m. – we had a nice dinner and enjoyable evening.

Tuesday 5/11/82

Didn't sleep much last night – coughed all night. Went for mail, took the Dziuk's back home. Went to cabin to dig outhouse hole bigger. Began lining it with green lodgepole to keep it from caving in. Cleared up more brush.

Wednesday 5/12/82

Finished lining the outhouse hole with lodgepole. Started building the floor and seat. Left at 4:30 p.m. To go with Frank to a combination birthday party for Lee Seacrest's son, and his wedding anniversary. I got to Frank's 5 minutes late – his watch was 10 minutes fast. He was upset. He sure has been edgy and hard to live with for the last couple of weeks. We left the party early.

Thursday 5/13/82

Went by store. Karen was having trouble installing the pipe in the well near her rental cabins. Helped her finish the job. Went to the cabin to work on the outhouse. Finished everything except for wrapping visqueen around the teepee poles. Chuck came by to help. We raked the wood chips from under the cabin. Went to the hostel to take a shower. Karen came by Frank's for a visit. Said she plans to go on a trip for a week or so and may not be back before I left.

Frank Evans' Outhouse

Friday 5/14/82

Went for mail – nothing. First time since I got settled here that I haven't had any mail. Helped Frank unload an ice box to put in one of his cabins. As he was rolling it out on the dolly, a wheel slipped off the planks and the ice box fell over. It wasn't damaged but broke a hole in the sheetrock. He got very upset – throwing things around and cursing. Something has been wrong for the last few weeks. He says he hasn't been sleeping at night. He has been overly, pushy, sharp and in general hard to get along with. I think he is having problems with his girlfriend Genny, but he won't say. I try to stay away from him as much as I can, but his attitude is still getting to me. I can see I'll have to have a talk with him or leave soon. Went to the cabin and spent the day hauling the wood chips and piling them up to burn. Moved over 60 wheelbarrow loads and I'm still not finished. Quit work about 4:30 p.m. and went to Kalispell. Had dinner with Karen – She was leaving for her trip.

Saturday 5/15/82

Spent most of the day washing clothes, getting supplies, having hand saw and chain saw blades sharpened for frank & Karen, running errands, etc. Back to the North Fork about 6 p.m. Had supper with Frank & Mark Ross. Worked on Frank's place till dark piling firewood I had cut for Karen and burning the brush. The wood was so dry that when I lit the pile it burned very rapidly, and was so hot it nearly got away.

Sunday 5/16/82

Finished burning brush I couldn't see to gather last night. To cabin to put visqueen on the outhouse. Cut up a few remaining logs for firewood. Tacked the insulation I had under the floor I had last put down. Put a coat on the outside of the front door also. Started hauling gravel from Vance hill to put around the pillars – Chuck Roxanne, Paula & Johnna Dziuk helped. Went to Frank's at 7 p.m. to have supper with him. Had a short talk with him about his problem. He still wouldn't say what it was but that he appreciated my concern. Got another load of gravel on the way up to the cabin. We were on our way to get another load of gravel when we got the truck stuck in the driveway. Worked for a couple of hours getting it out. It was long after dark. Took the Dziuks home & back to Frank's. Wrote a few minutes and went to bed.

Monday 5/17/82

Awakened by a phone call at 6:30 a.m. Went to the cabin to stack the firewood under the cabin. Stacked about 10 chords under the cabin. The Dziuk's, Chuck and Roxanne helped. Went to have supper with Frank at 7 p.m. Back to cabin to pile up more wood chips. They burned slowly, mostly smoldering & producing a lot of smoke. Back to Frank's about 11 p.m. He was talking on the phone – I assume to Genny. I didn't disturb him – I stayed outside. He talked till nearly midnight. I had on only a short sleeve t-shirt – it was getting cold. I didn't tell him I waited outside. He thought I had just came in – he seemed in good spirits.

Tuesday 5/18/82

Went for mail – took the Dziuk's to their house. Finished cleaning up the wood chips and shavings – over 100 wheelbarrows full in all. Raked the area around cabin & piled some firewood on side & back of cabin – it wouldn't all fit under the cabin. Began spraying and coating the outside of the cabin with linseed oil. To Frank's to eat at 7 p.m.Back to spray logs till 10 p.m. Went to the Hostel for a shower. I had sprayed all that was needed under the eaves but ran out of oil before I could finish the sides.

Wednesday 5/19/82
To Kalispell to get more linseed oil, to the bank to get money for my return trip and to wind up a few details. Chuck & Paula came with me. Back to cabin at 1 p.m. to finish oiling the outside logs. Installed a cable across the driveway with a padlock on it. To Frank's to eat at 7 p.m. Went to Frank Vitale's on Red Meadow road to return his sprayer. Visited for 1 ½ hours or so. Went to Peggy Gensler's to get some eggs, pay for some nails and visited till 12:30 a.m.

Thursday 5/20/82

Awaken by a call from Helen. She tried to connect me to Willie or Kevin – neither were there. Went to cabin to do some odd & ends jobs. Installed deer antler door handle inside door, cut board to cover picture window, installed a temporary door window, varnished inside door, put up bird house in top of tree, worked on trap door, finished tacking visquine on out house, etc. Roxanne, Chuck and Johnna came over. About midafternoon I went to take pictures of Rick and Windy Upton's son. He had a cold and wasn't up to it.

Spent an hour shooting ground squirrels on Frank's place. Back to cabin till dark. Went to Rob Fisher's to return a section of stove pipe and to visit a while. Went to Frank's to eat at 11:30 p.m. – to bed at 1 a.m.

Friday 5/21/82

Wrote a little this a.m., went for mail, Took Dziuk's to their house. Went to cabin. Put weather-stripping around door, made a door stop – coat hanger. Began organizing things I would leave and things I would take back to Louisiana. Took a few pictures. Rob Fisher came by for a visit. Went back to Rick and Windy Upton's and got a few pictures of their son. Shot a few gophers (ground squirrels) at Frank's place. Went to John Frederick's Hostel to help him change the piston on his snowmobile. He wasn't in. Karen was back from her trip. Their light was on so I stopped for a few minutes to visit. To bed 1 a.m.

Saturday 5/22/82

To cabin to cut rebarb rods to make braces for the stove support. Took them to Ron Wilhelm to weld for me. He was replacing the foundation at the store. Had a cup of coffee and back to cabin. Tacked pieces of tarpaper on the roof in places where it was coming loose. The tarpaper is shrinking and pulling through the tacks. I don't think it will last the summer. Don't have this problem in Louisiana so soon. The snow must have something to do with this. Changed oil in truck. And put spare tire on bracket beneath the truck. Cleaned Karen's chain saw, adjusted the chain, cleaned spark plug, etc. Filled up gas can and mixed oil in proper proportions. I had mixed nearly 5 gallons earlier, but had used it in cutting her firewood. Cleaned out the truck a little. Took everything off the bottom floor of the cabin and separated what was to stay and what was to go. Began cleaning and scraping the floor to prepare for the last coat of linseed oil. Went to Rick and Wendy's to finish taking pictures of their son, Andrew. To Frank's to eat at 7 p.m. Back to cabin to finish scraping and put the last coat of linseed oil on the floor. Worked by lantern light. Finished about 11:30 p.m., to bed at 1 a.m.

Sunday 5/23/82

Loaded snowmobile in truck and packed some food and clothes for a bear hunt. I was going to try to get over the Whitefish Divide to a place Cosmo said there were bear. Stopped by the store to get a bag of peanuts. Ron Wilhelm had my shovel and stove support welded. Took them to the cabin. Checked the setting on my gun at the Dziuk's on my way up trail creek Road. And had to cut several trees that had fallen in the road. Had to clear part of a road slide to get through. Dug my way out of several snow drifts until I encountered one too big to cross. Couldn't use the snowmobile because only parts of the  road were covered with snow. Rocks and gravel on the other parts. I walked the 6 more miles to the top of the divide. There were several snow slides along the way. Some were partially melted, but still were 30' or more high. Most were 50' or so wide. But some as wide as 100 yards. They took down all trees in their path. I followed the path of a black bear and a cub for a while. Didn't see any big game today. Walked back to the truck. Decided not to try to walk into the area Cosmo had marked on the map for me. It would take me all day to walk in with snowshoes. If I did get a bear, I didn't have the 2 days it would take me to pack it out. Drove down past the rockslide and found a place to sleep. Will hunt along the road by truck tomorrow. Today the mountains were serene, the air quiet. Life was scarce in the higher elevations except for the occasional moose track. I felt lonesome. Thought about the pros and cons of having a woman to share my life with. But even if it was what I wanted, where would I find a woman feminine and gentle enough to please me, yet rugged enough to follow me through life? The last few days have been clear, sunny and pretty. Birds have been singing and the hummingbirds were returning from their migration. For a week now the grass and flowers have turned the country green. Spring is in the air.

Monday 5/4/82

Spent the morning driving around Trail Creek Road and glassing the hills for bear. Stopped by Mark Rosse's cabin to visit awhile. Drove up Moose creek road to get a swift's nest that I had put under a bridge this winter. Drove up Center Mountain Road and glassed for bear. Didn't see any. Back to cabin around 3 p.m. Began packing and separating the boxes that I would leave from the ones I would take. Went to Frank's for supper about 7 p.m. Had a valve ticking in my truck engine. Adjusted it. Cleaned the ice chests, washed dishes and did general sorting.

Tuesday 5/25.82

Washed out the back of the truck and began loading it. Went to the cabin and began loading everything I was to take from there. The Dziuk's kids all helped. Did final chores around cabin. Bided the Dziuks goodbye – they will look after the cabin for me. Went to have supper with Frank. He had gone to whitefish and had left some spaghetti on the stove for me. Went to Hostel to see if John Frederick was there. We finally were able to change the piston on his snowmobile. Worked on it till 1 a.m. Frank and I visited Karen & Bettie till the wee morning hours.

Wednesday 5/26/82

Spent the morning preparing the snowmobile for winter storage, finishing John Fredericks snowmobile job, and changing the manifold to tailpipe gasket on Karen's truck. Wrapped the snowmobile in visqueen and stored it under the roof behind Frank's root cellar. It started raining this morning. Greased the truck. Spent the afternoon packing and loading the truck. It seems I am going back with as much stuff as I came here with. Went back to the cabin to drop off a few things I wanted to leave. Stopped by the store to bid Karen & Bettie goodbye. Karen was leaving to get supplies in Kalispell this afternoon. I told her I would have supper with her. Back to Frank's to finish packing. Left around 7:30 p.m. Went to bid Pandora goodbye. She seemed to know I was leaving for a long time. She just laid there with her head down in a pouting position with her eyes looking up at me. It was harder for me to say goodbye to her than any of the people in the North Fork. I will miss her the most – she has been my constant companion. Drove on to Kalispell and met Karen for supper. From here on I must change my thinking and my style of life.

Thursday 5/27/82
Had a good breakfast at Perkins. Stopped by the store to get a few cokes and snacks for the road. Bought another set of brake pads for the truck. The ones I had recently put on were coming apart. Drove to a baseball field just outside of Kalispell and changed them. Left Kalispell around 11:30 a.m. Drove to 3 a.m. Stopped at a roadside park just outside of Casper, Wyoming and slept in the truck. Encountered snow in Butte, Mt. and rain most of the way.

Friday 5/28/82
Awoke about 9 a.m. Had breakfast at a Shelby Truck stop. Called Helen from Denver, Col to have her relay a message to David and Alice that I'd be in Dallas sometime after noon tomorrow. Drove to 2 a.m. Stopped at a roadside park just east of Amarillo, Texas. The weather had begun to clear when I reached New Mexico. Went to sleep looking at the countless stare through the windshield.

Saturday 5/29/82

Woke up at about 9 a.m. It was a hot 95° today. The truck ran on the hot side of the gauge all day. Arrived in Fort Worth about 4 a.m. The engine was running hot but still within normal range when it suddenly quit in the middle of the freeway. I managed to pull it over to neutral ground between the lanes of traffic. I waited for about ½ hr. for it to cool off before I started again. It did this several times on the way to Dallas. I adjusted the clutch while I waited. Arrived at David's at 6:15 p.m. Kevin was there also. David and Alice were packing for their vacation. They were leaving in the morning. After supper Kevin told me he had gotten into trouble in January. He and some of his friends had stolen 3 cars. He was sentenced to 5 years' probation. He had hired and paid for his own lawyer and handled the whole thing himself. Perhaps this will jolt him enough to straighten out his thinking – we'll see. David and I talked with him till 2 a.m. about his life. David won't get much sleep tonight, but he felt it was more important to try and help.

Sunday 5/30/82

Up about 8 a.m. to bid David and Alice goodbye. Went back to sleep. Up again about 10:30 a.m. Went to Charlotte Karam's for lunch with her. We then went to a movie that evening. Kevin and I slept in her living room since David's air conditioner was off & she offered us a cool place to stay.

Monday 5/31/82

Had breakfast with Charlotte. Drove to Houston Texas. Stopped to say hello to Jane Mollett, but she wasn't home. Drove on to Lafayette, La – got there about 10 p.m. Kevin and I talked quite a bit about his life as well as about Lisa's problem. I was hoping he could help shed some light on Lisa's problems too. Stopped to say hi to the Hursts. Took Kevin to Helen's trailer. Lisa was there and came out. I told her hi, but found I wasn't overly happy to see her. I wanted her to see also that my way was the same as my words. I was aggravated that she had lied so much to everyone including me. I was disappointed with her and couldn't approve with her wayward life, and her unfairness. She went inside and started crying. I left and drove on to my mothers. Total mileage from the North Fork was nearly 2,400 miles. Had supper, unloaded the truck and went to bed. It was good to see my mother.

Tuesday 6/1/82

Today I end this book and jump back into society. I somehow feel I am surrounded by a bunch of little snakes all trying to bite me. I see a lot of work, and a lot of problems around and ahead of me. I am also acutely aware of the changes that have taken place. Prices are higher, buildings and roads are being constructed in Lafayette at a rapid pace. I notice the hum of electric things, the constant hum of the city (background hum), and a general noisy atmosphere. The most noticeable smells are of raw gas and mushy oil on the highways; cigarettes and perfume near people. I sense a slight constant tension in people. I feel a slight detachment from things I have known. The past year has given me a broader perspective. I have had hardships and losses, but nothing has been dehumanizing to me. I feel I have lived rather than just passed the time. My attitude and my life will undoubtedly change due to this experience.

The year is 2019. Jim Hale passed away in April of 2008. Polebridge is, and has always been a diamond in the rough. It's known for its long drive down a winding scenic dirt road. Skirting the banks of the North Fork of the Flathead River. As you drive down The North Fork Road. You start to enter another world, going back into time. Where there are no phones, no cell service or electricity, and no internet. Most everyone still has an outhouse standing in the yard. And every predator in the lower 48 still roams free. You are not at the top of the food chain anymore. The air is clear with a distinct refreshing smell. That I can only describe as smelling like Christmas. The rivers run so clear and fresh. That you can drink the water from it.

The cabin still stands in the same place. It has been through many of trials and tribulations. It survived the Red Bench Fire of 1988. Which almost wiped Polebridge off the map. And burned down most of the homes in Polebridge. Some people speak of the fire as being alive. And throwing giant fireballs high up in the air. And bouncing down the mountain like a basketball. Exploding every time it hit the ground. And seeing wildlife running for their life. As trees tumbled behind them. The sound of the fire was almost defining. And sounded like a freight train. Even Glacier Parks Fire Behavior Analyst were amazed at The Red Bench Fire. Saying they have never seen a fire behave like that. No homes were expected to make it. Most of the homes were burned. Not many homes survived the fire. The saloon, Hostel, and Polebridge Store barely made it. Having its own crews working to save them. The Red Bench Fire killed one firefighter. And injured 19. Over 700 firefighters were dispatched to The Red Bench Fire. Including Canadian firefighters. And all of the residents came together to help out. Most everyone fought the fire getting no sleep for days.

One of dad's closest friends and neighbor, Jerry Costello and his wife Sally. Took turns watering down their cabin for days. Watching the fire balls flying out of the fire grow larger and larger. As it came closer and closer to them. They did this for as long as they could. And were forced to evacuate.

I remember being with my Dad at Grandma's house in Louisiana. And my Dad receiving a call. He hung up the phone and went outside. He just stood in the middle of the driveway, staring up into the sky. I walked up to him to see what he was looking at. As I looked up at him, I could see that he was crying. I put my arm around him, as he tried to hold back the tears. I have never seen my father cry before.

When it was all over. 38,000 acres had burned. And residents describe the aftermath as "like walking on the moon". And the historic Pole Bridge was gone.

After it was all over. Jerry Costello walked around with a water tank spraying small fires that remained. Jerry went to check on Dad's Cabin. Not expecting it to be there. No one was there to water it down or do anything to protect it from the fire. It also had aged firewood all around the base of the cabin. And everything around the cabin was burnt to the ground.

The cabin was still there!
The fire came a foot from all sides of the cabin and stopped!
"Devine Intervention" is how I would describe it.

Outhouses of the North Fork Polebridge, Montana USA

PHOTOS BY: JAMES W. HALE
(THE CAJUN MOUNTAIN MAN)

Old Homestead about 1/4 mile south of Polebridge Store and Meadow

362

Corrine Spindel lived here for a while on Moose Creek Rd.

Ethyl Newton Homestead

"Rat Haven"
Jimmy Little's

Tom Reimer's Outhouse

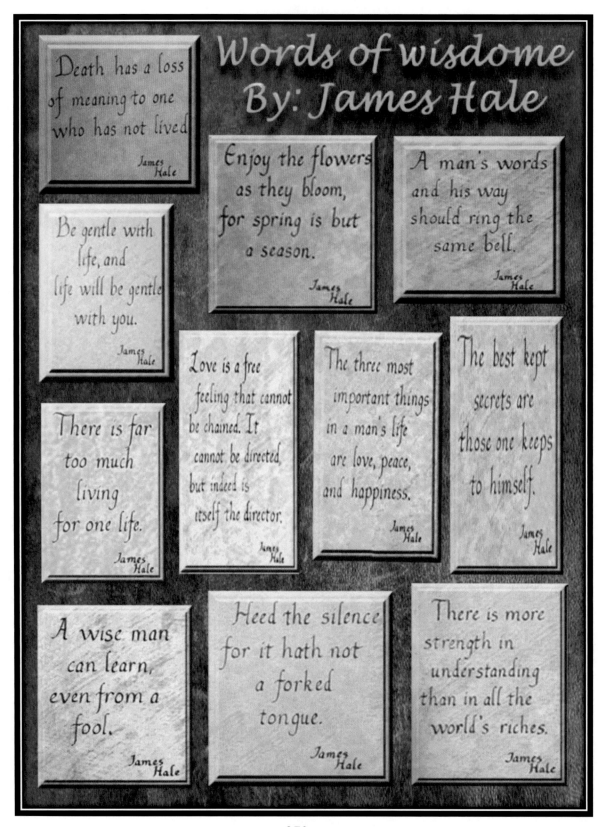

Words of wisdome
By: James Hale

Death has a loss of meaning to one who has not lived
James Hale

Enjoy the flowers as they bloom, for spring is but a season.
James Hale

A man's words and his way should ring the same bell.
James Hale

Be gentle with life, and life will be gentle with you.
James Hale

Love is a free feeling that cannot be chained. It cannot be directed, but indeed is itself the director.
James Hale

The three most important things in a man's life are love, peace, and happiness.
James Hale

The best kept secrets are those one keeps to himself.
James Hale

There is far too much living for one life.
James Hale

A wise man can learn, even from a fool.
James Hale

Heed the silence for it hath not a forked tongue.
James Hale

There is more strength in understanding than in all the world's riches.
James Hale

370

Lisa Hale Gallagher Presents...The Works Of

James W. Hale

(The Cajun Mountain Man)

James Hale, a native Louisianian, known for his photographs of the Atchafalaya Basin. Despite having Macular Degeneration, takes spectacular photographs of a mountain wilderness in Polebridge, Montana. Where wild predators far outnumber people, streams run crystal clear. And trees split like rifle fire as the mercury plunges to 40° F below zero. James Hale has had progressive macular degeneration since he was a kid. His form of macular degeneration is rare and untreatable. Inherited from his fathers before him. And passed on to his son Kevin Hale. Who always says "We see much better than people with normal eyesight. While your eyes focus on what is right in front of you. Our eyes were taught to focus on our peripheral vision. And see the larger picture". But they can all still "shoot a flea off a dog while it's chasing a chicken" with extreme accuracy. In this book James Hale's daughter, places his photos along with his diary to tell the story of "The Cajun Mountain Man"

In the words of James W Hale...

Have you ever had a dream – just to get away from it all - to find a place somewhere back in the woods – to stay for a while?

Well, I had such a dream. In the spring of 1981, I set out to make these dreams come true. I took a leave of absence from my work, packed my clothes and headed for the remote wilderness of Montana's northernmost mountains – home of the grizzly bear, the gray wolf, the American bald eagle, and as tales tell it, even Sasquatch. Some 20 miles from the Canadian border, on a high bluff overlooking a wild and scenic river. I found a spot. Here, with little more than a hand saw, a hatchet, and an 80 year old draw knife, I built my first log cabin – and for a year I became a mountain man. I lived my dream.

Made in the USA
Coppell, TX
19 December 2021

69505637R00221